Peasant Movement in Uttar Pradesh

(From 1857 to 1947 AD)

Peasant Movement in Uttar Pradesh

(From 1857 to 1947 AD)

Dr. Geeta Yadvendu

Delta Book World
New Delhi - 110002

First Published in 2018
ISBN : 978-93-85719-04-2

Published by **Abhishek Goel** on behalf of
Delta Book World
G-4, Prahlad House
4832/24, Ansari Road
New Delhi - 110 002 (India)
Ph. : 011-47072321
E-mail : deltabookworld@gmail.com

PRINTED IN INDIA

Preface

It is difficult to express the helps and encouragement which I have received in completion of this work. I do hereby take the privilege to put forth my sincere thanks and regards to Dr. Sugam Anand, my guide and Professor in Department of History, Dr. B.R. Ambedkar University at present. I take great pride and consider myself fortunate to work under his honourable and able guidance and supervision. The direction and guideline set by him along with Dr. Pratima Asthana, former Vice- Chancellor of Gorakhpur University cannot be enumerated. She has been my true hepled during the whole time I have been put through this work. I am gratefully indebted by her selfless act of providing me best of her ideas regarding this work.

I am extremely thankful and owe a debt of gratitute to the employees of Central Library, Dr. B.R. Ambedkar University University, Agra Institute of Social Sciences, and Archeological Survey of India, Northern Jone, Agra, for providing me valuable sources without which this work will not have been taken the present shape and figure. My thanks are also due to the staff of National Archives in New Delhi and State Archives in Lucknow for providing me relevant papers and record.

I am also grateful for the helps and inspirations to my parents, brothers, in-laws and to my husband Mr. Ajai Kumar whose blessings always remains with me in my life.

Geeta Yadvendu

Introduction

The present work is a study of Peasant Movements in Uttar Pradesh under the British rule. The region today known as U.P. comprised the two provinces of Agra and Oudh annexed gradually by the British. The acquisition of Benaras region in 1793, was the first step in this regard. The Nawab of Oudh was persuaded to cede, in addition to the area of north of Benaras, the Central Doab and Rohilkhand. The Company conquered the "Upper Doab" in 1803 and Bundelkhand in 1817. When the empire of the Company covered the northern India, they divided it in "Ceded and Conquered Provinces". The "Ceded provinces" were such territories as ceded by the "Nawab Wazir of Oudh" to the East India Company. The "Conquered Provinces" were the territories annexed by the Company from the state of Daulat Rao Sindhia. The Nawab of Oudh and Daulat Rao Sindhia had taken possession of these territories in the days of the decline of the Mughal empire. The British originally viz. Allahabad, Cawnpore, Gorakhpur, Moradabad, Bareilly, Etawah and Farrukhabad comprising the Ceded Provinces and Agra, Alighrh, northern Saharnpur and Bundelkhand comprinsing the "Conquered Provinces" and afterwards the "North-Western Provinces". When the British gained control over the Ganga-Jamuna region it opened up the prospects of tapping its vast agricultural resources. Dalhousie finally annexed the Oudh in 1856. Wajid Ali Shah was the last Nawab of Oudh. After 1857 the administration of the "North-West Province" and of "Oudh", functioned peacefully. They were amalgamated under a single head in 1877 and the territories were renamed as "The United Provinces of Agra and Oudh". After independence in 1947 it was again renamed as Uttar Pradesh.

This sighty region has been called as the heart of India. The entire area or U.P. has been agricultural since time immemorial.

During the British rule, acute problems were faced by the peasantry of this region. As a result, they suffered grim poverty. They burst out in revolts from time to time. The peasants were poor, helpless and illiterate. It is surprinsing that they always expressed their anger against the alien exploitation and revolted sharply. They also stood against the curel landlords and the moneylenders.

The region known as U.P. presents a glorious history of peasant struggles in protest of British exploitation. The peasantry of this province though uneducated, daringly opposed the cruel and exploitative policies of the British. In the great Revolt of 1857 millions of these impoverished peasants participated. Many historians believe that the Revolt of 1857 was a civil movement fought united by soldiers and peasants. In the 20th century, United Provinces emerged as the first big centre of peasant movement. Peasantry of this province launched a constant struggle and strengthened the Indian National Movement.

In fact the peasant movements in United Provinces later become a separate and had unrelated origin. The patronage they received from educated classes, inspired them to be organized. In this sense, peasant movement in United Provinces, was a child of Indian Nationalism. The direction to them came from the Home Rule League and the Indian National Congress both. The movement from below responded to the politics from above and the initially sporadic nature of Kisan Sabha activities were given a direction by the developing trend of national political events in India.

The "United Provinces Kisan Sahba" was established by Indra Narain Dwivedi in February 1918. After the Delhi session of Inidan National Congress, a keen interest in the activities of "U.P. Kisan Sabha" arose and they began to concentrate on the problems of the peasants.

In 1920 peasant Jhinguri Singh and Baba Ramchadra started a movement in Pratapgarh and Rai Bareilly districts of United-Provinces. After the activities of Pratapgarh district in late 1920, these peasant struggles started to be better organised. Gouri

Shanker Mishra and Pt. Jawahar Lal Nehru were closely connected with this movement. In 1920, they formed "Oudh Kisan Sabha" with Baba Ramchandra as its chair person. Madari Pasi started "Eka-Andolan" (Unity move) in 1921-22. This movement started in Hardoi, Baharich and Barabanki regions of eastern U.P. By the June 1922 "Eka-Andolan" was cruelly crushed by the British government.

After 1920, these peasant struggles started to be better orgainsed. The peasant started to get inspiration from Mahatma Gandhi. The feelings of anti-imperialism now merged with the nationalism of non-cooperation movement. The two great leaders, Baba Ramchadra of Fyzabad and Madari Pasi of Hardoi organized and united the peasantry to spread the national consciousness among their class.

In the Agra district of United-Provinces, the peasant revolted in 1920 and many of them joined the non-cooperation movement of Mahatma Gandhi. They stopped paying taxes and readily accepted the punishment by the government. Seth Achal Singh was the inspring personality to the peasants, who assumed their leadership.

In April 1936 "All India Kisan Congress" was formed in Lucknow. Swami Sahajanad was its first President and N.G. Ranga was the Secretary. Both of them gave full attention to the basic problems of the peasantry.

A larger part of the peasant movemets in United Provinces have been related to Oudh. Oudh, as a region, has a historical significance of its own. Twelve districts of eastern U.P. comprise Oudh which were ceded to the British time to time. Dalhousie finally annexed Oudh in 1856. The peasantry of Oudh was better orgainzed than the peasantry of Agra province. They fought therfore with more efficiency against the discriminating policies of the foreign authorities.

Under the leadership of Mahatma Gandhi, the agitation started by Indian National Congress reached the rural areas because he deepened the base of Congress among the masses and invited the peasants to join his movement.

In the Post War (1919-21) period, the growth of peasant struggles in United-Provinces increased. The Chouri-Choura episode (February 5th, 1922), the withdrawal of non-cooperation movement of Mahatma Gandhi, became a watershed in the history of peasant movement. Heroism, militancy and readiness ot struggle became the temperament of the rural poor people so much so that it strucked terror in the hearts of the ruling class. It added strength to the national movement. It also proved the truth that the lowliest and deprived peasants possessed the energy to rise above and march ahead on the path of patriotism and glory.

An attempt has been made in this work to study the causes, the actual events and the effects of the peasant movements in U.P. The movement became very strong in Oudh due to the revenue policies, agrarian structure and the dual exploitation of the peasantry at the hands of alien Raj and oppressive social groups as landlaords and moneylenders. The life study of character and personality of the great leaders of this movement who worked to organize the poor and illiterate peasantry of the province has also been studied in this work.

The impact of these peasant movements on the socio-economic life of the peasantry of the province forms an important aspect of the present work. A comparative study of the peasant movement and the non-cooperation movement in the light of contradictions within the anti imperialistic struggle, becomes the researcher's necessary quest. The interesting phase is that the peasant movement amalgamated in the national movement for freedom. However it was considered to be the right panacea of all ills and evils prevalent in the province. The researcher has attempted this study in an impartial manner and style. She has taken the help of original records and consulted the revenue records of these villages. The struggle of the peasantry gave it the form of a majority revolt against the handful of alien rulers and became a constant source of irritation for the British administration in India.

The researcher has also depicted the sad plight of the peasants under the three-sided exploitation ot the British authorities, the neo zamindars and the money lenders. The morale of the peasants remained high even in days of cruel treatment and harsh oppression.

Contents

1

The Beginning

(Outbursts in Various Directions)

The peasant sturggle against the British rule started when they tried to change the agrarian sturcture of the country after the acquisition of Diwani rights in 1765. Beginning with the "Sanyasi Vidroha of 1772." These struggles widely spread over a period of nearly one and a quarter century. The revolt to the pesants often occurred at many places at a time.

The term "Peasant Movement" and "Agrarian Movement" refer to all kinds of collective attempts of different strata of peasantry either to change the exploitative system of the British, or to seek redress for particular grievances, without necessarily aiming at overthorwing the system. These two terms used interchangeably, refer to all kinds of movements of resistance violent or non-violent, organized by the tillers of the soil in India.

Kathleen Gough writes, "In India peasant revolts have been common in British period and more than 77 revolts are clearly discemible."[1]

In all the areas in which the first war of independence (1857-60) spread the peasants played a heroic part, suffered terribly, displayed great military skill and achieved numerous victories. Many groups of peasants fought to destroy British rule over an area of more than 500,00 square miles.[2] The British changed their strategy and often persuaded the new land buds to side with them.

---

1. Kathleen Gough, "Indian Peasant Uprisings", Economic and Political Weekly special number, August, 1974 pp 1391-1412
2. S.B.Chaudhary, "Civil Rabellion in the Inidan Mutinies, 1857-59". World Press Calcutta 1957, p. 32.

After 1859 the British rule and military preparedness became stronger than ever before and rural upper classes of landlords were either crushed totally or coopted by the British through concessions. There are many types of these rural struggles. These movements had a history of at least 120 years since the British established in India. The earlier protests of peasants were rather unorganised and took place at a regional level and in small groups of the semi-conscious masses. It was after 1918 that the peasants began to develop political consciousness. They took part in organized national struggles and tried to build up their own organizations under their own flag and programme. The peasant movements before 1918 were not organized and had only limited economic aims. Occasional struggles broke out in different parts of the country at different intervals due to severe famines, or other agricultural miseries. These struggles were against the zamindars, moneylenders and the administration. There were many other reasons of these protests. Excessive land revenue and other innumerable ceases were imposed on the peasants. The burden of such taxes became too heavy. The British administrators were interested only to increase their collections year after year. The possession of land became mere a burden than an asset. Between 1770-1897 there were several disastrous famines all over India. Those of Rayalseema were the worst. In the famines of 1770, 1896 and 1897 millions of poor Indians died for want of food and water. The relief given by the government was scanty and the alien government succeeded in weakening them. But on the contrary, this increased the revolutionary capacity of the peasants and workers. They decide to struggle against their miserable condition and revolted from time to time in different parts of country. Their revolts were directed against the misrule and the negligence of the British.

Indigo Cultivators Strike

The famous Bengal Indigo strike of 1860 was the first large and successful strike in inida, Indigo, a plant growing by Indian cultivators yielded the dye necessary for bluing the cotton cloth.

With the growth of the modern textile industry in Great Britain in the late eighteenth and early nineteenth century, there was a great expansion in the demand of this dye. Thus Indigo trade became a rich source of high profits for the East India Comapny in India. Retired officers of the East India Company, and young upstarts, many of whom were previously slave drivers in America, acquired lands crop on a large scale as a plantation industry. They used to force the tenants to grow and sell the Indigo at a very low price under a system of great oppression. They were forced to grow and sell at a very low price for the British textile industry, to the exclusion of most other crops.

Peasants resistance against this exploitation was emerged in Nadia, Barasat and Pabna. In place of mute protests, the peasant decided to take action on a large scale in April 1860. All the cultivators of Barasat sub-division under took what was probably the first general strike in the histroy of Indian peasantry. They declared themselves against the opperssion of the planters and refused to sow the Indigo any more. The planters felt shocked in a memorandum submitted in April 1861 to Sir Charls Wood, secretary of State for India. Mackintey, Chairman of the "Landlords and Commercial Association of British India" declared that, the State of the mofussil had now (July 1860) become one of entire confusion. The debtor were not contented with rejection their debt and contracts, but they even conbined to drive their creditors and employers out ot the country, and thus to get rid of all Europeans in the province, to retain the property they had seized and cancelled debts and obligations due to Europeans.[1]

On April 1860, over 2000 peasants, drawn from the 52 villages collected at the Pabna district and wounded a magistrate's horse. The Indigo cultivators strike was a unique event in the history of Indian peasantry, this strike covered large districts of Pabna and Nadia and in Barasat sub division had declared the first general strike which soon spread to Jessore, Khulna, Rajshahi. Dacca, Maldah and Dinajpur, approximately most of Bengal.

1. Indigo Cultivation in Bengal Parliamentary Papers (1861), Vol. XLV, PP. 70-71

Even before the birth of Mahatma Gandhi, the peasants in these districts had followed the path of general and non violent strike. The Inidigo cultivators of these districts separated by so many miles, undertook this united action, if the area cover which the strike spread and the number of peasants particapating in the area taken into consideration, it surpasses the campaings of Mahatma Gandhi at Champaran and Khaira and by Sardar Patel in Bardoli.

The Government however was not to be easily moved to rush troops against the revolutionary Indigo cultivators. They had not forgotten the memories of great Santhal insurrection of 1855-56 and the memories of rebellion of 1857 were too fresh in their minds. The Indigo cutivators had succeeded in winning the sympathy and support of other sections of population. The urban middle classes and many intellectuals of Bengal were in favour of the struggling peasants. Even some of the missionaries expressed sympathy with this struggle.[1]

Harishchandra Mukhopadhyaya, Girish Chandra Basu, Dinabandhu Mitra, Sisir Kumar Ghosh and many other well known intellectuals of Bengal were in favour of the peasantry. Dinbandhu Mitara wrote a higlly popular play "Neel Darpan 'exposing the oppression and injustice of the planters in Mollahati.

Due to all these factors the government could not dare to take any action against the revolters. Instead of sending tropps to break the general strike and quell the uprising, the government announced the appointment of a commission to investigate the whole system of Indigo cultivation in India.

J. P. Grant, Lieutenant Governor of Bengal also suggested the government not to take strong measures to crush the uprising of Indigo Peasants.

The Government issued a proclamation in the form of instructions from the Hon. Ashley Eden, Chief Magistrate of Kalawah sub-division, in which it accepted the rights of cultivators

1. Indigo Cutlivation in Bengal, Parliamentary, Papers(1861), Vol. XLIV, p.4, cited by L. Natarajan.

to sow any crop they liked without any inter ference by the planters or any one else.[1]

This was a complete victory for the Indigo cultivators. As a result of the strike, Indigo cultivation was largely forced out of these districts to Bihar and U.P. The Indigo cultivator's strike of 1860 was in fact the first large scale non-cooperation movement, in the form of a complete strike, in the modern Inidan history, the British understood that they shall not have and easy sail in India.

Maratha Peasant Uprising

In Deccan the peasant revolt of 1875 was joined by water-carriers, barbers and even house-servants of moneylenders. The slump in cotton prices, after the end of civil War in America hit the Inidan Kisan hard. Their debt burden became very heavy and so the Maratha peasants rose against the money lenders, who with the help of courts used to constantly oppress them.

This revolt covered Poona and Ahmednagar districts and spread upto Gujrat. Thousands of peasants assembled in public gatherings, in market places and decide to boycott the claims of money lenders and seize their documents. They raided the houses of money lenders, destroyed documents of debts and even killed some of them. After three weeks the troops against the boycotters, hundreds were arrested in each centre, and the government levied collectiove fines over them. The riot was finally crushed. However, the government felt the necessity of relief of the peasants and passed the Deccan Agriculturists Relief Act. in 1879.

Bengal Tenants Outburst

In 1870, the Bengal tenants were hit hard by the economic depression accentuating their general poverty. The Bengali Zamindars prospered under the protection of the permanent ssttlement at the cost of the industry and the hard working peasants. Production of jute has been a special gift of nature to Bengal. This came to be in great demand in the world.

---

1. Indigo Cutlivation in Bengal, Parliamentary, Papers(1861), Vol. XLV, p.4, cited by L. Natarajan, 1953.

It enriched only the Zamindars and the production of jute benefited them. They in turn imposed upon them more rents. Legal and illegal imposts were multiplied and Nazranas premiums were heaped upon peasants. For tightening the alliance between the British and Zamindars during the revolt of 1857 even the courts decreed that the land itself belonged to Zmindars and the peasants were only tenants at will. There was no limit of exploitation and torture of peasants by the Zamindars. Just about 1870-80, the economic depression had also contributed its share towards the growth of poverty of the peasants.[1] Suffering under all these miserable conditions majority of the pesants began first to fall into arrears or rent then to be threatened with the loss of lands and eviction from their home steads. And so thousands of peasants refused rents, disobeyed the dictates of the curts. They stopped their eviction and finally started fighting with whatever weapons were available with them. A regular state of anarchy came to prevail in large parts of Bengal and Santhal country side and a reign of terror was set afoot. The rising was quelled by the government which however appointed an enquiry committee and subsquently enacted the Bengal tenatcy Act in 1885.

Punjab Descontent

The Peasants of Punjab also agitated and threatened to revolt to prevent the rapid grabbing of their land by the urban moneylenders for failure to repay debts. In 1890-1900 the Sikh, Mohammadan and Hindu peasants of Punjab could not tolerate the superiority of money lenders, conferred upon them by the British Civil Laws. In Punjab as a result murders of moneylenders began to increase. Taking these as signs of revolt, the British Government quickly passed the Punjab Land Alienation Act in 1902-03. Prohibiting the transferring of land from Kisans of other classes for more than twenty years.

The Government also passed the Saharanpur Rules, according to which the Land Revenue should never exceed 50 per cent of net income from the land, either at the original settlement or at any resettlement condition.

---

1. W.W. Hunter, Annals of Bengal.

South India in Agitation

The peasant of Krishna and Godavari region, and the Karnataka and Rayalseema peasants also revolted several times from the beginnings of 19th century to protest against the high increase in land revenue imposements, the neglect of irrigation facilities and the brutal methods of tax collection, G. Lakshminarasu Chetti organized a grand constitutional agitation against the Madras tortures and succedded in getting it repealde and this saved the south Indian peasants from being put to several cruel and inhuman tortures for failure to pay taxes.

The South Indian peasants used the method of Satyagraha by abandoning their lands and villages and migrating to the neighburing Indian state. As a result, the Government had to climbdown and agree to a reduction of their tax burdens in order to persuade them to return their land and villages.

Peasant Struggles after the Emergence of Gandhi

Emergence of Mahatma Gandhi on the scene of Indian National Movement was the start of a new awakening among the masses of this country. After returning from South Africa, Gandhiji made the experiment of his principles of Satyagraha of Champaran (Bihar) and Kheira (Gujrat). Gandhiji succeeded in gainning the aims of the struggles but not at a very vast scale. This is also true that a bread based agrarian programme was not presented by Gandhiji to the peasants.[1]

But this is also true that, for the first time the nationalist recognised that peasantry was a class suffering due to British feudal lords and the imperialitst government. They felt the need of launching a struggle on their economic demands. Mahatma Gandhi tried to give a new, dynamic and revolutionary tendency to the peasant struggles. In 1917-18 he familiarised the peasants of Champaran in Bihar and khera in Gujrat with his new weapon of Satyagraha, an open non-violent, organised politically alive revolt against British injustice and exploitation. He trained the

1. S. B. Chaudhari, Peasants' and Workers' Movement in India 1905-1929, Peoples publishing House, New Delhi, 1971, p.25

masses to reomve its internal fears and to face the harassments of imperialism without fear.

Champaran Struggle

The Champaran stuggle of peasants was launched under the leadership of Mahatma Gandhi and Dr. Rajendra Prasad in 1917-18. It was a struggle against the indigo planters, most of them were Europeans, who forced the local Bihari peasants to grow Indigo against their will. The poor peasants also forced of paying higher taxes and illegal exactions.

Gandhiji initiated the method of Satyagraha and non-Cooperation, and open non-violent revolt against the indigo planters and land revenue collectors respectively. He started sharing the sorrows of the peasants. Thousands of suffering peasants flocked round him and detailed their woes. This struggle reflected the spirit of revolt against exactions and oppression to which the poor indigo cultivators were exposed at the hand of European planters. In his report submitted for the persual or Mr. Maude, the chief secretary of the Government of Bihar, on 12 May 1971, Mahatma Gandhi stated the grievances of the Champaran peasantry in detail,

"Indigo may now be defined as an obligation presumed to attach to the ryot's holding under coercion. It is inconceivable that the ryot would agree to an enormous perpetual increase in their rents against freedom from liability to grow indigo for a temporary periods, which freedom they were strenuously fighting to secure and honourably expecting. Under the Tinkathia system the ryot has been obliged to give his best time and energy also to it, so that very little time has been left to him for growing his own crops, his means of livelihood, inadequate wages have been paid to the ryots, and even boys of tendeage have been made to work against their will. There can be no doubt that the latter (Planters) have inherited a vicious system. They with their trained minds and superior position have rendered it to an exact science, so that the ryots not only have been unable to raise their heads above water but would have scunk deeper still had not the government granted some protection. But that protection has been meagre and provokingly slow and has often come too late to be appreciated by the ryots.[1]

The struggle was not directed only against the European planters but it was also a reflection of ryot's dissatisfaction against the ruling classes which had a racial ties with the planters. The intellectual personalities organized the peasants of Champaran for fresh struggle. Besides Mahtma Gandhi, Dr. Rajendra Prasad, Brij Kishore Prasad. Muzharul Haq and a number of other people belonging to the intelligentsia inspired and organised the peasants of Champaran against the injustice created by European planters. Raj Kumar Shukla was one of those who was filled with a passion to wash away the stain of indigo for the thousands who were suffereing.[2] He wrote a letter to Mahatma Gandhi on 27 February 1917, "In a corner of India, the inhabitants of this place (Champaran), who have the proud privilege of being under the comfortably cool share of British umbrella, are leading their lives like animals suffering from all kinds of miseries."[3]

When the main sturggle started in April 19 the statements of more than 800 tenants from abut 850 villages in Champaran against 60 factories of the European planters were recorded under the supervision of Mahatma Gandhi. The cotinuous recording the these statements gave a new political consciousness to the peasants and fearlessly they complained against the European planters. It was a new political awakening among the rural masses of India.

The enquiry committee submitted its recommendations and the outstnding features were that Tinkathia was to be abolished. The tenants were allowed to hold their landsfree from any obligation to grow indigo. Proper arrangements to prevent unnecessary litigation between the peasants and the planters were promised by the authorities. On 29 November 1917, Mr. Maude introduced the Champaran Agrarian Act was approved and assented by the Governor-general of India on 1 May 1918, this was the final stage

1. Home (Pol.) Department, Government of India 1917, file No. 438-41, p.4.
2. Rajendra Prasad, Champaran and Mahatmel Gandhi, P.O. Delhi 1955.
3. Freedom Movement in Bihar, Government of Bihar, 1957, Vol. 1, p194

of sucess of the Peasant movement in Champaran which generated a new confidence among the peasants and they recognised the power of a united and organised struggle. This was also the success of Mahatma Gandhi to attract the peasants into the main stream of the National Movement. Mahatma Gandhi used it in the development of nationalism among the rural masses of India. but acording to the critics this struggle gave only a partial relief to the peasants. professor N.G. Ranga, who was critical of Gandhi's leadership remarked." Just as the earlier Congress agitation led by R.C. Dutt against temporary settlements did not embrace the exploitation of our peasants by Zamindars, so also this agitation led by Mathtma in Champaran did not lead up to any fight against the main causes for the terrible poverty and sufferings of Champaran peasants namely the execessive rents and exorbitant incidence of debts, it dies strike us rather significant that both he (Gandhi) and Rajendra Prasad should have remained need for liberating peasants from its cluches"[1]. But he also accepted that, this Champaran Satyagraha Movement of 1917 during the First World War had the excellent result of awakening not only the Bihar peasantry, but also the general public of India to the tremendous revolutionary potentialities latent in the bosom of our peasants.[2]

Kheira Satyagraha (Gujrat)

After the Champaran Satyagraha of Bihar, Gandhiji organised the Satyagraha Movement of peasants in Kheira against the collection of land revenue which they could not pay due to failure of crops. The Bombay Government blindly demanded the payment of land revenue ingoring the fact that peasants were not in the condition to pay. In March 1919 the Khaira Satyagraha was launched under the leadership of Mathama Gandhi, Sardar Patel, Indulal Yagnik, N.M. Joshi, Sanker Lal Pareekh and many others who were also persented at Champaran. In this strugle the public workers tried to establish contact with the actual life

1. History of Kisan Movement by N.G.Ranga and Swami Sahajanand Saraswati, All Inida Kisan Publications, Madras G.T.

2. Ibid.

of the peasantry. Vitthal Bhai Patel raised the issue in Bombay Legislative Council. In their inquiries the leaders of the movement found out that the demands of the peasantry for suspension of the revenue assessement of the year was fairly justified. But the authorities refused the demands of the peasantry. Then Mahatma Gandhi exhorted the pattidars to resort to Satyagraha. in this movement the intelligentsia effecitvely played a role in seeking to "rid the agriculturists of their fear by making them realise that the official were not the master' but the servants of the people, in as much as they rceceived thier salalries from the taxpayer."[1]

The British goverment used repressive measures. Notices of fines and penalities were issued to the peasants and their standing crops in the fields were attached. despite these repressive measures the majority of the peasant agitators remained stubborn and continued in their struggle. The movement ended only when the officials accepted the peasants demands. The agreement arrived between the officials and representatives of the peasants laid down that the well to do pattidars would pay up the rents and the poorer ones would be granted remissions.

Starting of Peasant Pariticipation in the National Movement

Upto the last phase of first World War peasant unrest in India, especially in the form of Champaran and Khaira struggles, acquired a radical character. After that the peasants participated with full strength in non-cooperation and Khilafat movements. No doubt, Mahatma Gandhi was the only personality who recognised their problem and difficulites.

He changed the feudal character of Indian National Congress and tried to make it an organisation of people , rich or poor, rural or urban. under his leadership the mass of peasantry realised that their stuggle against feudal exploitation had better chances of success if it was organised under the guidance of nationalist leaders. They thought that they could understand the interests of rural masses

1. M.K.Gandhi, "The Story of My Experiments with Truth" Ahmedabad Navjivan Publishing House, 1945, P. 334.

better due to their education, knowledge and intellectuality and that without proper leadership imperial powers could easily abolish their movements as it did in the revolt of 1857. This was the fact that the peasantry of this country could understand and realize well. The intelligent section of the peasantry also came to realise that the end of the feudal exploitation could only be possible, when the alien government left them free for their own home rule. The development of this outlook gradually made this class, the champion of self rule which was being already advocated by the nationalist leaders and intellectual classes of this country.[1]

On December 1918, nearly 700 peasant delegates from around Delhi area attended the Congress session of that year and collaborated alongwith the delegates of the intelligensia in the demand of self rule. One of the tenant delegates Choudhary Peeru Singh addressed the session, "It is said that only the educated people sat together to demnd Swaraj. it is not so. We also demand it. I have said "demand" accidently. We want to get Swaraj, we are not beggars. Our brethren have sacrificed themselves in Europe for which they are being praised all over the world. I am a jat and a cultivator and a resident of the district which has supplied twenty - one thousand recruits. We are all with Pandit Malaviya. We want that we should mangae our own affairs. but will never get Swaraj till you carry the cultivations with you."[2]

Peasant Movements after the First World War

After 1919 Indian peasantry cultivated national consciousness which started to spread among them during the Champaran and Khaira struggles. it was the great non-cooperation movement which succeeded in drawing in the effort of millions of peasants with its magical slogan of, "Swaraj in One Year", into its orbit. The Indian National Congress gave a slogan of non-payment of land revenue which had a magical effect. The peasants interpreted the political struggle for Swaraj in terms of a struggle against the heavy land tax. Other sections sympathized and supported their

1. Report of the Special session of the Indian National Congress held in Delhi, 1918, p.116.
2. Ibid.

participation in the movement. It was the starting point of a section of the Indian peasants to join an organized political movement.

During this period of non-cooperation movement, struggles which were not organized by the Congress also broke out. Those were the struggles in the Guntur district, Karnatak and Awadh Rent Act of 1921 which paritally met demands of the peasants was enacted by the government. Millions of peasants, believing the end of British Raj, boycotted the rents and revenue and began to carefully watch the political developments. They were fully inspired by Mahatma Gandhi. But Mahatma Gandhi suddenly withdrew the whole non-cooperation movement and left millions of peasants, and the whole country in mid-air. Lakhs of peasants were exposed to long term of imprisonment, torture and other kinds of oppression by the British. Their Zamindars penalised them. Those millions of peasants who were participating in the movement with the hope of a better future suffered terrible disappointment and frustaration.

Gandhi's decision of withdrawing the non-cooperation movement terribly disappointed not only the rural masses but also the national leaders, intellectuals and everyone sturggling for country's freedom. Young militants like S.A. Dange, E.M.S. Namboodaripad, M. Singaravelu Chettior, Pt. Nehru expressed their complaints against Gandhiji's decision without any hesitiation. Criticising the Gandhian technique of independence, S.A. Dange worte, "So Gandhism requires a change in human nature of purification, which in due course will destroy the necessity of the present system of life". Destroy vanity, love of show and there will be no necessity to engage wage-earning slaves to produe silks and luxuries. Destroy fear and love of power, wars will stop and militarisms and government will melt. Destroy the devil with in man and out side nature if incongruties will die out. Lenin might as well answer to this "Destroy the universe and god himself, who is the cause of all this, and everything will stop a madman's reasoning and impossibility".[1]

1. S.A. Dange, Gandhi vs Lenin, Bombay, Liberty Literature Co., 1921, pp. 33-34.

On 28 December 1927, on the occasion of the Madras session of the Congress, Jawaharlal Nehru, complained, "since the failure of the non-cooperation movement the congress had been drifting to middle class of Babu politics and was losing the support of the masses. It was important for them to form somekind of an organisation which would keep the National Congress upto the mark and also prepare the country, not only in a republican ideal but also in a right republican ideal."[1]

Due to this the peasants faith in Gandhian leadership was shaken. The withdrawal of non-cooperation movement seemed as the betrayal to the masses. This vacillating conduct of the Congress led to the growth of independent peasant movements in the different parts of the country and the peasants decided to fight for themselves.

The Moppla Revolt

Mopplas were moslems by religion. Mostly they were agricultural workers otherwise tenants or the most depresed section intermediary labdholders. The Nambudry Brahimans were the actual owers of the land. They had absolute rihgt of electing any intermediary peasant or any of the actual cutivators. These intermediary peasants were also Hindu, the Nairs and they helped Nambuddie. These two classses of land holders (Nambudaiers and Nairs) exploited the poor Mopplas, the most depressed section of intermediary land holders, with or without cultivation. Naturally, an agitation sprang up in the wake of the religious revivalist movememt, towards the beginning of the middle of 1921. Though the main grievances of the Moppilas were related to agrarian discontent, yet in the absence of a scientific rational and secular leadership the movement passed in to the hands of reactionary and Orthodox powers. In their traditional way these Orthodox religious priests turned the strugge, which was against exploitation, torture and injustice in the form of a communal strife by forcible conversion of a considerable number of Hindus. After giving religious touch to the movement, the Moppilas could not sustain

1. The Indian Qunrterly Registrar, Calcutta, Vol-III, July-December, 1971

their resistance for long they were isolated morally from the rest of Hindu India and surrounded on all sides by overwhelmingly superior and more powerful imperialist forces which blocked all routes of arms supply. More than 3,000 Mopplas died and several thousand were wounded.[1]

Contrary to the principles of non-cooperators, the Mopplah rebels has turned to armed struggle against the imperialists and landlords. The Congress expressesd deep sorrow at the violent methods adopted by the revolters.[2] The Indian National Congress still harped on the strings of non-violence.

The Congress Working Committee pointed out that the government report had exaggerated the harm caused by the mopplah uprising and underestimated the cruety of the authorities. "In the name of peace and order".

Thus the Mopplah uprising, was a link in the chain of the anti-colonial agitation of the masses during the postwar years. it had very great significance, not for the peasants alone, but for the national liberation movement as a whole. It encouraged the will of the peasantry to stuggles for its rights and stand on their own legs.

Bardoli Satyagraha

Vallabh Bhai Patel, organised and led the Bradoli peasants against the resettlement, enhancements proposed by government. The Bardoli peasants rose against the unjust enhancement of land revenue sought to be imposed upon them by the Bombay Government. They were led by Sardar Vallabh Bhai Patel and assisted by Mahatma Gandhi. Under their inspiring guidance, the peasants braved all risks, faced with courage the loss of their believed cattle and ancestral lands and even risked eviction from their villages. At last they triupmhed over the government in 1929. Their limitless sacrifices and discipline and determination were the chief factors which ulimately won for them their complete success. At last the Bombay government appointed and impartial

1. The Life of Nationalities, Moscow, 1922, No. 117, p. 12
2. Sukhbeer Choudhary, Peasants and Workers Movement in India, p. 101

enquiry committee. The Committee gave its decisions mostly in favour of the peasants. This victory of Bardoli peasants put courage into the Inidan peasantry and evoked their hopes of being able to struggle against the injustice and exploitation. Again in 1930, when Mahatma Gandhi gave the call to the people to rise against imperialism to achieve national independence. The Bardoli peasants again refused to pay taxes, faced the auction, sales and eventual loss of almost all their lands and refused to have any relation with government. They had showed marvalleous strength under the leadership of the great Sardar. In 1937-39 when Congress formed the ministry, Sardar Patel managed that all their lands were returned. The peasants gained their initiation again in both economic and political Satyagraha.

Vizag Revolution and Sitaram Raju's fight

The tribes of Vizag agencey fought a two-year war against British imperialism under the leadership of Sitaram Raju. In one of the broad backs of the Eastern Ghats, in the Jeypore Zamindari and on the borders of the Narsipatam taluk, Alluri Sitrama Raju, a kshatriya of west Godavari district, enacted one of the most revolutionary drama in the life of modern India. Sitaram Raju went there and saw the sufferings of those ignorant but brave people, at the hands of forest and excise officials. Those hill tribes were not allowed to carry on their 'Podu' or 'Jungle' cultivation. They had to pay too many taxes upon so many of their activities such as gathering fuel, grazing their cattle in forest etc. so that their very traditional mode of life was threatened by the government. When all his appeals of mercy were in vain, Raju decided to fight against the injustice. The rising, soon became a violent revolution and it was suppressed at great cost to human life on both sides. The British Governments made a merciless and ruthless use of fire and iron. The revolutionary peasants were fighting for their legal rights, for free use of the forest land and produce. Rapidly they increased their demands and desired to claim swaraj for the whole of the country. The British Government was very cruel towards these brave and militant tribles. It used all the modern weapons and killed thousands of the Kuya and Savasia people.

Their trouble doubled when their noble and resourceful leader Raju was killed. Most of their other leaders were either killed or sent to jail and the masses faced great reprisals. Yet the sprit of resistance of these hill tribes did not die. It only awaited another inspired leader and a suitable opportunity. This become clear in the August 1942 revolution when again these people revolted and showed their anti-imperialist spirit.

Peasant Rebels in Different Indian States

The peasants of a number of Indian states were involved in revolt between 1937-46 against the horrible conditions of life. The sufferings of the peasants in the Indian States were even more intolerable and they had to bear the burden of the continually accumulating illegal abwabs and the imposts.

The Indian peasants began to protest these exploitative taxes and decide to rise in revolt. At first the Loharu Patiala and Nabha peasants revoted. They abondoned their villages and run into the neighbouring forest. They were struggling for rent reduction. After three months struggle, some partial success came their way. A number of Satyagraha compaings have come to be organised against so many unjust laws and imposts. The struggles against Karnataka Forest Laws in 1921 and 1934, the rent exactions in U.P. and Bihar in 1921 and 1931-33, the anti resettlement compaigns of Godawari and Krishna deltas and number of peasant struggle against landlords of Venkatagiri (1931), Tsudumu and Munaga (1939), were orgainsed in the south. There were also the land Satyagraha in Bihar (1939), The anti-Zaminadari fight in Bengal and Andhra and Canal duties strugle in the Punjab and Bengal (1939), the jute prices struggle of 1937-42 and the Debt Relief Agitation also cover the discontenment of the people.

There was a revolt of the peasants in Jaipur, Gwalior and Udaipur, against their local Thakur and other feudal lords. They were led by late Jamnalal Bajaj, a merchant prince and great follower of Mahatma Gandhi. They achieved victroy on their economic front. The Udaipur revolt was put down cruelly, but the forced labour were abandoned by the British.

During the half of 1946, the Hyderabad peasants rose against their local feudal chiefs, the Deshmukhs. The Coummunists and Congressmen provided the requisite leadership, but the communists tried to elbow out the Congressmen and achieve an "closed shop' for their organisation, With the result the ranks of the peasants divided a large section of the middle classes and the merchants were forced to join hands with the state authorities in order to save themselves from Communist repression. The state authorities and their local fedual and other allies perpetuated many horros on the peasants of Warrangal, Nalgonda and Bihar. Lootings, repings and murders of peasants became the order of the day. It was stopped only when states, people organisation and the Andhra Congress began to champion their cause. After that the state called a halt to its campaign of repression. But this freedom from feudal lords of the states was won at great cost by the state peasants. The sufferings of Hyderabad peasants were of a sterner type. the state people were victimised by the Nizam of Hyderabad and his ministry, that consisted the Razakars, a gang of powered Moslems. The state people fought heroically against those super power. The tribal people (Koyas of palvanchatulu). The Kisans of Nalgonda, Warrangal, Mahboobnagar districts struggled heroically against the state's campaign of violence and repression.

At last the statemanship and strong 'Police action' conducted by Sardar Patel, the hero of Bardoli Peasant Satyagraha of 1928, forced the Nizam to surrendar. With his fall came down the Razakars terror and the power of the landlords.

The liberation of almost the whole princely order and the consequent liberation of 70 million states peoples and their attainment of democratic government was the biggest achievement of post colonial India achieved by Sardar Patel, the Kisan Satesman.

August Revolution and Peasants

Indian peasantry played the most heroic, dynamic and effective role during the 1942 Revolution. Peasants rose spontaneously and simultaneously, they upset the means of transport of the British war machine, captured police stations and other local offices of British Government. Wherever they succeeded in overcoming the local government forces, they proceeded to establish their Panchyats. In United Provinces, Bihar, Bengal and Maharastra and Tamilnadu they established their rival government to the British. The most famous achievements of the peasants Were witnessed in Midnapore and Satara districts where for years, the British were unable to regain their control over whom regions consisting of the masses of peasants. In the 20th century and the 1942 revolution the peasants showed their firm decision to achieve political power and they were no longer content with mere looting and occasional display of their discontent and fury. They did not harm private properties, ordinary individuals and attacked only on the government agents and properites. The peasants became the central figure of 1942 revolution. They esatblished their separate panchayats for poliitical, administrative and indicial purposes and worked with harmony and efficiencey. In the villages of Satara district these panchayas did remarkable work. They made and enforced laws. They collected taxes and cesses and adminstrated public funds. The peasants joined them with national affairs and freedom struggle. Wherever there was a struggle, the peasants of whole of India become interested in it, tried to help the sufferers in every possible manner. The Mandasa state subjects, the Orissa state subjects, refugee camps, the Bengali flood victims, the Rayalseema famine stricken peasants, the Malabar peasants and so many other were helped on all India basis. All India Peasant Congress played a remarkable role to knit all the peasants together under the aegis of a national peasant unity. But it was only the Mahatma and the Indian National Congress who laid the foundation for the growth of the new consciousness among the Indian, familirized them with the potent idea of their national unity.

Thus the Indian peasants have a long tradition of armed uprisings, reaching back and least to the initial British conquest and the last decades of Moughal Government. for more than 200 years peasants in all the major regions repeatedly rose against landlords, revenue officers, moneylenders and alien government and mostly with success.

Although peasant revolts have been wide spread, certain areas have an especially strong tradition of rebellion. Bengal was ever a hotbed of revolt, from the earliest days of British rule. The most successful revolt of the recent period occurred under irregular conditions which are unlikely to be repeated. The Tebhaga revolt took place three years after a famine had killed three and a half millions Bengalies. In Telangana in 1947 the change of government created an emergency as the Nizam of Hyderabad refused to accede to the Indian Union, and it was some time before the Indian government decided to invite the state and mop up both the Nizam forces and communists.

Four major fights apart from the first war of independence (1857) were put up by our peasants. Although these early struggles were not modernized and fought in a primitive way, they have resulted in considerable concessions from government. The masses revolted during the later nineteenth century didn't have political consciousness. There were neither political organisatioins nor class orgainisations at that time. These movements were fought on a regional level and early freedom fighters and Congress did not take interest in peasantry. The Indian National Congress did not lay as much stress on the need for relief for the peasants, during 1905-19 as it did on the needs of Inidan industrialists. It did not try to adopt a bold and forward policy with regard to the protection of peasants. The national leaders continued to press for the establishment of permanent settlement of land revenue, for abolition of salt tax, and excise revenue, but they could not totally succeeded on behalf of the agriculturists. Even they remained silent about the fate of the crores of Zamindari tenants of U.P., C.P., Orissa, Bihar, Bengal and Assam. Lord Curzon's chanllenge to Romesh Chandre Dutt, an economist, patriot and an ex-president of the Congress, that it was the government which had done more to protect tenants from the capacity of Zamindars, remained unanswered probably because the then leadership of Congress was more capitalistic in its culture, and most of the members of Congress was more capitalistic in its culture, and most of the members belonged to the Zamindars or the Industrialist classes of India.

It was only Mahatma Gandhi who tried to give a new energy and revolutionary tendency to the peasant struggles since his emergence on the Indian political economic scenario in 1916. He joined the Congress with the problems of rural masses and gave it a universal charcater. Actually it was he who initiated the national awareness among them and made Indian fully prepared for conducting their own movement against the British Raj.

2

Relevant Issues in Uttar Pradesh

The region, today known as Uttar Pradesh was annexed by the British gradually after 1795. The acquisition of Benaras province in 1793, was the first step in this regard. In 1801 the Nawab of Awadh was persuaded to cede in addition to the area of north of Benaras, the Central Doab" in 1805 and Bundelkhand in 1817. When the empire of the Company spread in northern India they divided it in "Ceded and Conquered Provinces". The Ceded Provinces was the name given to the territories cede by the "Nawab Wajir of Oudh" to the East India Company and "Conquered Provinces" to the territories annexed by the company after conquest over Daulat Rao Sindhia. The Nawab of Awadh and Daulat Rao Sindhia had taken possession of these territories in the days of the decline of the Mughal empire. The revenue administration prevalent in these territories on the eve of British conquest was originally developed by the Mughals.

The British basically divided these "Ceded and Conquered provinces "into twelve districts viz. Allahabad, Cawnpoore, Gorakhpur, Moradabad, Barrielly, Etwah and Farrukhabad comprising the "Ceded provinces" and Agra, Aligarh, northern Saharnpur, southern-Saharnpur, and Bundelkhand comprising the "Conquered Provinces". The districts bearing these names at present are much smaller in area since several new districts have been carved out of them for various reasons. The British rapidly swallowed many territories. In 1835 they renamed the "Ceded and Coquered provinces" as the "North West provinces" The control of Ganga-Jamuna doab opened up prospects of tapping its vast agricultural resources. Oudh was finally annexed by Dalhousie in 1856. Wajid Ali Shah was the last Nawab of Awadh. He was sent to Calcutta and the Company settled a pension for him. After the failure of the "Great Revolt of 1857" the Crown administration of "North West Province" and of "Awadh", functioned peacefully side by side. They were amalgamated under a single head in 1877 and the territores of "North-West Provinces" were renamed as the "North-West provinces of Agra and Awadh." After 1902 it was further renamed as "United Provinces of Agra and Awadh" and in 1937 its name was shortened as "United Provinces". The region was given the name Uttar Pradesh after independence on the proposal of Rajrishi P. D. Tandon.

When the British annexed the region the rural society of the province was of a complex nature, divided into caste and communities. There were several horizontal social layers with all together different rights and claims.[1] They all lived peacefully in the same village accepting their status given to them in the society according to the social norms.

By the mid-nineteenth century, rights of cultivating occupancy were largely hereditary in the majority of districts of "Noth-West Provinces." These hereditary rights were not equally distributed within a community.

There was a marked disparity between privileged and under privileged farmers. The dominant members of a local community granted subordinate right of access to farmers beneath them on the social-scale. Most of the farmers had to pay due return for the recognition and maintenance of cultivation rights. The Haq - kasthkari was levied on each harvest by their maliks or masters. A malik was one who possessed a milkiat, which means "possession" or "Mastership". These Maliks were the dominant-members of a community whose power was derived from the source of wealth and degree of prestige they commanded. They were known by their additional "Super imposed" status or by their official title of Mokuddum, Zamindar or Talukadar.[2]

1. H.S. Maine, Village Communities in East and West (London) 1895, p. 123.
2. G. Campbell, "The privileges over land", Indian Economist, December 31, 1874, p. 120.

Mokuddams, or village headmen were the lowest authorities in this official ranking. They were the first link in the chain which bound the rural communities to the government. Most of the Mokuddams were privileged farmers, the most respectable men of the community.

Above the Mokuddams there were the Zamindars. They were regarded as the most powerful authority over a local community and they enjoyed a very respectful position in the rural society. They had to supply the government with a stipulated amount of revenue and they had to arrange the agency for its collection. the area from which a Zamindar had rights to collect revenue was known as his mahal, or estate. All farmers living or cultivating within the area of his estate were subordinate to the Zamindar, authority in some degree and they could easily exploit them, if they wanted.

By the mid-nineteenth century in most of the NWP districts Zamindars were the most powerful authorities who dominated over the local affairs. But the situation was different in Awadh, where Zamindars were the subordinates of Taluquadars. One Taluqa of a Taluqadar consisted of several Mahals or estates[1]. The cultivators had to pay heaviest charges to all these authorities.

The annexation of Indian territories by the British created a sudden change in this established situation. Almost overnight, they brought about a complete political change. They implimented their own ideas in collecting the land revenue. They ruined the handicaraft industry, which was as mighty as agriculture. In the absence of other opportunities for investment, the acquisition of land became an attractive proposition for the neo-rich who were in very advantogeous postion under the British.

When the Britigh annexed Awadh in 1856 the Taluqadars had established themselves as middle men between the cultivators and the state. The term Taluqadar means the holders or a Taluqa (a group of villages, as a head mentioned). He was engaged to

1. Elizabeth Whitecomb, Agrarian - Conditions in Norhtern India, Vol. 9, 1860-1900, p.41.

collect the land revenue from his Taluqa and had to send it to the government.[1]

During the Mughal period the land revenue administration was systematized and the central authority dealt directly with the cutivators through the officials of the state. These officials were known as collectors of revenue. Their activites and operations were conducted by the government with a view to checking their oppression and malpractices. The disintegration of the Mughal power and the gradual decline of the central authority increased the power of the provincial governors. The checks on the oppression by the collectors of revenue gradually lessened and their authority increased considerably. They took advantage of the decline of central authority and prevailing anarchial condition. They arrogated to themselves the status of Taluqdars which was recognised by the decaying central authority. As soon as the power of central government was weakened. The Taluqdar class resemed authority over their Taluqas with the supprot of armed men they maintained[2]. In this manner, the vicious circle persisted for long.

At the end of eighteenth century Nawab Sadat Ali Khan, the king of Awadh, tried to oppose the growth of large Taluqas. He tried to engage his officials directly with village occupants for land revenue collection. This policy was adopted to check the Taluqdars who "absorbed a larger proportion of the rental than the petty Zamindars."[3] The policy failed as the central power had become weak and the Taluqdars had acquired military power and they were able to defend themselves. By 1856, Taluqs had grown beyond their original limits and Nawab Wajid Ali Shah had lost all control over them.

The region of Uttar Pradesh then comprinsing the two provinces of Agra and Awadh, was gradually annexed by the British. The province came to have at least three different tenurial

1. Asia Siddiqui,Agrarian change in a Northern Indian State, 1819-33, Oxford, 1973, p.44.
2. W.H. Moreland, The Revenue Administration of the United Provinces, Allahabad, 1911, p. 166
3. H.C. Irwin, Gardens of India, Vol.2, p. 160.

arrangements. In the district of Banares and small areas adjacent to it, a permanent settlement of Bengal type had been conducted with Zamindars and the individual land owners.

In the Agra province, acquried by the British mainly between 1801 and 1817, the Mahalwari settlement was prevalent in rural areas.

When Awadh was annexed on the 13th February 1856, there started a new chapter in the histroy of landlord peasant relations. Within a period of three years two divergent principles were adopted regarding the land revenue settlement in Awadh. The first settlement adopted immediately after the annexation was slightly provillage proprietors, while the other that came in 1858 not only undid the work of the former settlement but also currently ruined the peasants. They became poor and helpless, surrounded by poverty and indebtedness, due to exploitative measured of the alien rulers, they suffered a lot.

It is interesting to note that in the early phase when the British gained power, Zamindars and Taluqadars had right to collect revenue from the inhabitants of any given area. for the British, land revenue was the primary source of income and they used to increase it at regular intervals. They required help in this process because they had to settle it with the persons who were the owners of land. In England the owners of the land themselves had to pay the land revenue. But in India, the revenue was paid by the Zamindars and other middlemen who were not the owners of the land. it is strange that the British recognised these middlemen, as the owners of land, the cultivators are left to their mercies. They felt that it is easy to collect the revenue through a limited number of Zamindars rather than from innumerable cultivators.[1]

Their objective was to collect more and more money with minimum expenditure. Thus the British adopted the Zamindari system in India to provide a social base for the colonial power in strengthing its own power. They extended individual ownership of land as a means to retain their hold on the growing dominions.

1. A. R. Desai, Social Background of Indian Nationalism, p.39.

But in case of Awadh, the British were not ignorant of the corrupt practices to the local Talukdars. So, immediately after the annexation they adopted a policy to check the growing power of these Taluqdars. In the adjoining provinces of Agra, they adopted a different poicy regarding land-revenue. They set aside the officials, who acquired quasi proprietary rights and a hereditary postion, during the decline of Mughal power. The Taluqdars of Awadh were more powerful to their counterparts in Agra. In other areas they enjoyed a powerful almost place to the government. In order to check their power, Lord Dalhousie, the Governor- General of India, had directed the resident of Awadh, General Outram, to have the settlement made with the "actual occupants " of the soil without the interposition of Taluqdars as middlemen. Thus at the first summary settlement in 1856, out of the 23,543 villages held by the Taluqdars before annexation, only 13640 were settled with them and 9,903 were settled with persons other than Taluqdars.[1] But the measures adopted, could not fully uproot the Taluqdars. Their discontent towards the British government came to be seen when they joined the revolt against the British in 1857. The revolt was very strong and most wide spread in Awadh. The Taluqdars joined the revolt in hope of regaining thier lost property and status. The peasants joined hands with the Taluqdars in opposing the "Company Raj.[2] According to Baden Powell those villagers supported the Taluqdars during the revolt due to their hatred for the alien rulers whom them called Ferangis.[3]

The British expected some assistance from the village occupants, with whom they had conducted the first settlement. but "not an individual dared to be loyal to the Government.[4] Hence, after the revolt the British changed their policy and returned to the natural leaders of the people and policy settled with the great Taluqdars in Awadh and made them equivalent to the Zamindars.

1. H.C. Irwin, "Gardens of India" London, 1880, p. 160.
2. Kathleen Gough, Indian peasant Uprinsings, Economic and Political weekly, Bombay, special number, Aug. 1974, p. 1391.
3. Baden Powell, The Land System of British India, Vol. 1, Delhi 1974, p. 202.
4. Freedom struggle in Uttar Pradesh, Kanpur 1957, Vol.2, p.358.

After the revolt, the first step which the government took in March 1858, was to proclaim a general confiscation of propreietary rights in Awadh. Soon after Sanads (doucuments of entitlement) were granted to the Taluqdars giving them full propreitary rights on certain conditions which included among them the obligation to "Promote Agricultural Prosperity?[1] In 1859 Canning promised the Taluqdars the protection for their loyalty. Sands were followed by a second summary settlement which was conducted for three years beginning from 1 May 1858. In this summary settlement, out of 23,564 villages of Awadh 22,658 were settled with Taluqdars and only 906 villages settled with other persons.[2]

From this Second Summary settlement the British regained the faith and loyalty of Taluqdars. They felt strong enough to warn the peasant proprietors that they should not oppose Taluqdari settlement.[3] The settlement also assured the Taluqdars of their hereditary rights and dignity. Thus the Taluqdars emerged as a distinct class who were loyal to the alien government. They became much stronger than ever before as a rental collector.[4]

The new settlement was a political bargain enforced to avoid confrontation between the British and the Taluqdars and speed up the process of establishing the British. They recognised the fact that their class and status depended on their loyalty towards the British rule and they missed no opportunity to prove their loyalty.

In March 1861, the Taluqdars established, "The British Indian Association of Awadh" with the object of taking every lawful and constitutional measure to help Her Majesty's administration in Hindustan and especially in Awadh. Finally the Taluqdari system was established in the region and the taluqdars became the favoured few of the Britishers. The men who were merely the "middlemen" had been firmly established after 1857 as lords of the

1. S.N.A Fadri History and Status of Landlords and Tenants in the United Provinces, Allahabad 1931, p. 163.
2. Papers Relating to land Tenures and Revenue Sttlelementsin Oudh, p. 83.
3. T. R. Metcalf, The Aftermath of Revolt, p. 149.
4. Pioneer December-2, 1868.

land and enjoyed the "landlord's paradise". This system brought to an end all the flexibility which had characterised the agaraian set up before the advent of the British Raj. In this system the peasant was deprived of the ownership of the land and was soon to loose his occupancy rights too.

From 1871, a number of taxes were assessed on land in addition to the land revenue. If the land revenue was 50 per cent of the rental, the total asesement on the soil including the new taxes came to be 56 percent, or 58 percent or even 60 per cent, of the rental. This new system came as a bolt from the blue for the poor peasants. Whatever the nature of the agrarian society, however the basic structure of the agrarian society, remained fundamentally the same throughtout the region of U.P., though apparently it looked different. Besides there were generally one or more subordinate layers of holders of the rights in land. They paid rents to their immediate superiors for the land, they held and often cultivated, as tenants, sub-tenants or worse. In addition to these groups, there were the landless labourers and various marginal groups whose rights were not at all maintained and left ignored. They were occupiers of land without title or occupirers without proper consent.

The system of subordinate tenant layers did not exist in all the villages. some times the village co-sharers (Pattidars) or brotherhood (bhaichara), who paid the revenue, themselves cultivated the land. But even in the Mahalwari settlement, possibly because of defects in the original settlement, there were left many peasants whose rights were accouired by the strong landlords and they were left weaker and exploited. The non-cultivating, rent-collecting landowner soon became a common figure and also the exploitation and torture of weaker peasantry became very common in the field of agriculture.

The Genesis

With the annexation of the provinces, there bagan a period of peasant exploitatioin in them. It is notable that in the territory directly governed (not princely estates), the highest total revenue was derived from the United Provinces. Around 1921, the land revenue demand was higher in United Provinces than the rest of British India average. Though the rate of revenue seems to be not very high in comparison with other areas; it was actually higher due to the personal demands of the middlemen or the Taluqdars[1].

The land-revenue demand of the province of Awadh rose steadily between 1860 and 1900. In 1890-91 and 1900-01, the land revenue demand registered the greatest increase. It was very high when compared to the other Zamindari area, Bengal, which had a conspicuously low rate as given in the permanent settlement. When compared to Madras or Sind, Raiyatwari areas, the land revenue demand in Awadh was almost equal to that in the Raiyatwari areas. Even in the years of the agrarian distrubances of 1921-22, the land revenue demand reached its highest point between 1870-1920, there was a rapid increase in the population of Awadh. In 1869, the average population density per square mile for Awadh was 474.[2] And it increased to 504 in 1921.[3] The districts where the Kisan Sabha Movement was in progress, the density of population was very high. These were Faizabad, Pratapgarh, Sultanpur, Barbanki and Rai Bareili, Lucknow had the greatest density of population in the districts of Eka Movement there were increase in the pupulation.

Between 1881 and 1911 there was a steady growth in population in Rebarelli and Sultanpur districts. This population growth affected the tenancy structure more than anything. Macandrew observed in 1872, "The main cause of the poverty of lowest class of tenants and agricultural labourers is , beyond a question the density of the population and the disinclination of the people to move to a new spot; for dense as the population, there is land enough in the district itself to give them a large measure of relief, if they only break it up. But they multiply their numbers and subdivide their holdings till famine puts a limit to both.[4]

1. Agriculturel statistics of India, 1921-22, pp.45-47
2. Mazi Hayat Sidiqui - Agrarian unrest in Norhtern India, p. 49.
3. Census Report of 1921 for the United Provinces, part II, p. 451
4. Raebareli Settlement Report, 1872, p.76.

Between 1915-1916 and 1921-22, in United Provinces there was no significant change in the area under the plough. the growth of population only served to increasing the pressure on land because there was no other area of employment and productiveity of the soil remained stable. The increasing revenue demand and a practically static per acre cultivation led to the fragmentation of holdings.

In the eastern region, Benares and Gorakhpur were the most over crowded, and they suffered most from the sub division and fragmentation of holdings. Awadh was the area worst off in terms of the rack renting and exploitation of the subordinate classes. The glaring cause of this exploitation was the favoured position of the Awadh Taluqdars.

The British increased complications in agriculture with them increased the tensions among the various classes of society. The tensions started from the annexatioin of Awadh and increases with the growth of peasant movements towards the end of the second decade of 20th century. The span of sixty years between 1860 and 1920 was interrupted by a mirage of security from arbitrary eviction. Through the Oudh Rent Act of 1868 the Govt. gave a legal shape to the Taluqdars. They became busy enhancing the rents of tenants holdings. The Rent Act of 1868 did not recognise any other tenant right except that the tenants who held proprietory rights within thirty years of the annexation should receive occupancy rights.[1] The Act also debarred the courts from interfering in the matter of rents payable by tenants at will[2].

The state had left free the Taluqdars in Awadh to make their terms with tenantry. The Act was a fatal below to the peasantry of Awadh. The Pioneer rightly commented that," the Awadh Rent Act failed to protect just those tenants who, most urgently needed its protection.[3]

The agrarian structure in Awadh - at that time was as under :

(a) The Taluqdars, Proprietors

1. Imperial Gazetteer of India, Vol. XIX, p. 291.
2. Revenue and Agricultural Department, April, 1884, National Archives of India, Rev. A., PNo. 16.
3. Pioneer, 14-3-1872

(b) Zamindars, Sub-proprietors

(c) Pukhtadars, Under-Proprietors

(d) Occupancy tenants

(e) Tenants at will

(f) Agricultural labourers.

A little margin existed between the tenants at will and the agricultural labourers, because once a tenant at will was evicted, the only avenue left open to him was to work as an agricultural labourer. The taluqdars became more confident and powerful to obtain for themselves all the profits that could be extracted from the land, they enhance the rents and the ejectments became a very common practice. The landlord became most powerful authority to make bargain annually and enhance rents without any fear of central authority. The most simple and effective instrument to deal with the tenantry, in their hand was the instrument of ejectment. The primary motive to the landlords was to bring the tenants to their terms rather than to ejecnt them. Evictions followed mainly in those cases where the tenants refused to agree to their terms. Between 1880 and 1884, 29 per cent tenants had been actually evicted, 26 percent accepted enhanced rents and reamined undisturbed. The rent charged with them had no relation with the productivity of the soil. Occasionlly irregular methods of eviction on enhancement of rent were used. To ascertain the extent of the rents, the Lieutenant-Governor setup an inquiry in 1872. In several districts there was no limit of the rising extent.[1] From Barabanki district it was reported, "In the case of low caste tenants and a strong landlord, the former submit either to ejectment or enhancement without the formality of a notice, and it is these low caste tenants on whom rents are imposed limited only by the possibility of payment.[2] A Ziledar frankly said against Harrington who was reporting from Sultanpur district that, "I arrange the rents on the principle of getting as much as I can."[3]

1. Awadh Revenue Administration Report (ORAR), 1880-81, p.-65.
2. Deputy Commissioner's Report from Barabanki
3. ORAR 1880-81, p. 75-76

This kind of increase in rents made the tenancy more dependent on village Banias or Mahajans. A sad condition of general indebtedness was created. Not only Banias or Mahajans but also Brahmins and Thakurs adopted the trade of money lending. They exploited the poor peasantry for whom there was no other option than to borrow from the money lenders.[1]

As a result indebtedness of tenants caused indebtedness of agricultural labourers. The moneylenders charged heavy interests and there was a feeling of heavy bondage. The conditions were so worst that any person belonging to lower castes as Chamar, Kurmi, Kori or Lodha, who received debt from a rich farmer, landlord of Mahajan became a bonded labour for whole life or till he repaid his debt.[2]

The Oudh Rent Act of 1868 proved totally inefective in regulating the affairs of the landlords and tenants.

Between 1880 and 1886 the question of the tenants right reappeared in Awadh. There were allegations and counter-allegations made by the supporters and opponents of the prevailing land-tenure system. H.C. Irwin pointed out the demerits of the current land system in Oudh. But Raj Kumar Savradhikari came out in defence of the Taluqdari system in 1882.[3] Irwin maintained that the most urgent need in Awadh was the security of tenure for the cultivators, and suggested a system of thiry year leases for the tenants-at-will.[4]

The English press also pointed the defects of the exisiting law and urged an amendment in the present system.[5]

The Awadh Rent Act of 1886 was passed and the most important change was with regard to the tenure or tenants all will. The Rent Act of 1886 had granted to all tenants at will in Awadh the right to hold their land undisturbed, at an unchanged

1. PD. Reeves (ed.) Sleeman in Oudh, Cambridge, 1971, p.74.
2. Oudh Gaetteer, Vol. 1 1877, p. 145.
3. Raj Kumar sarvadhikari, p. 272.
4. H.C. Irwin, The Garden of India, London, 1880.
5. Pioneer, 12-2-1883

rental, for seven years, as recommended by Empire. After that period, the government succeeded in limiting the rate or ejection and rent enhancement. The tenant after that could not be either ejected or his rent could not be enhanced till the end of every years period the Rent Act further limited the extent of this enhancement which now could not exceed 6-1/4 per cent of the previous rent, a new category of statuary tenants was created by the Oudh Rent (Amendment Act). The Agra Tenancy Act of 1926 adopted the category for Agra. Statutory tenants had security of tenure for life, their rents could be enhanced only once in ten years at rates agreed upon by both landowner and tenant or in court, and the heir of such a tenant continued to hold the land on the some terms for five years after his death. Most of the former tenants at will in Awadh qualified for these rights.

The Awadh landlords succeeded in overcoming the new legal hurdles from the late 19th century onwards. They not only ignored the law to a large proportion but also instituted a new system of unoffical taxation. This was the nazrana, or premium paid by a tenant to be admitted or re-admitted to a holding.

The landlords were habitual to lead a life of luxury. They always neaded money for their extravagances. They didn't have any interest in agricultural prosperity and had no sympathy for their tenants. For the fulfilment of their money demands they always remained in search of new ways to squeeze money by legal as illegal means. Soon they discovered defaults in the new Rent Act[1] and found an opportunity to acquiese as much as they liked.

In Lucknow for a lease of one bigha or land, carrying a rent of Rs 10, the tenant had to pay nazrana or Rs. 10, to the landlord with the Patwari and Ziledar (landlords agent) getting rupees one each[2]. Because of the fear of eviction tenants had to pay high nazranas and abawabas. If they tried to refuse to pay, they were ejected from their holding.

In Agra province, by contract, an 'occupancy right, heritable

1. Nazrana : An extra premium on rent taken as gift payment.
2. Radha Kamal Mukherjee, Land problems in India, Calcutta, 1933

though not transferable, with rents at customary rates and certain statutory controls on enhancement, had been long recognized for some categories of tenants. The Act of 1859 first formalized the possession, laying down that continuous possession and cultivation of a holding for twelve years entitled the Agra tenantry was in a strong situation legally. The area held by occupancy tenants increased during the first three decades of 20th century. With that there was considerable improvement in the economic position of stable tenants. While prices rose by more than 100 percent between 1900 and 1920, the rents of occupancy tenants rose by only 20-25 per cent. On the other hand for the non-occupancy tenants the registered rent rose by about 70 percent during this period. In Agra alone, where unwritten and illegal demands were rarer than in Awadh, such tenants (non Occupancy) were paying 110 per cent more in 1930 than they had paid in 1900. In 1928 the occupancy rent in Agra was said to represent only 10 percent of the produce value.

But the position of the ordinary tenant in Awadh was certainly worse unless he was protected by legal authorities.

The western divisions of the province like Agra and Meerut were more advanced than Awadh, in terms of urbanization and industrialization. These divisions of western UP and the Doab had a relatively low share of agriculture, in the work force, rarely over 66 or 67 per cent.

On the other hand, the divisions of eastern UP and Awadh generally had some 80 per cent of their work force in agriculture. But as a whole out of 46 million people in UP in 1921, 89 per cent lived in rural areas.[1] Throughout the first half of this century agriculture accounted for 74 to 76 per cent of the provinces's work force.[2] In this vast rural population land owner held a strong posititon and dominated the other classes. For UP as a whole we have a picture of great landlords dispersed over many districts. They possessed a good deal of land and lived almost completely

1. Census of India, 1921 United Province of Agra and Oudh, Vol. XVI, part I, Report (Allahabad) 1923.
2. Ibid.

on rents, other cesses and usury. There was a much larger number of small landlords and rich peasants, spread all over the province. They held fairly substantial and secure holdings and lived an luxurious life.

Below this categories were the middle peasants who lived on the produce of their own land and on family labour, employing only seasonal and part time labour. They had small land and other resoureces, which were insufficient to feed their families and as such they worked even outside as labourers.

These lower classes contained a high majority of agricultural population. In 1944-45 nearly 10 milion people, that is over 81 percent of the 'agriculturists' were counted in this category of peasants.

There was rarely a sharp distinction between one class and the other in rural society, in UP, the distinction between poor peasants and landless labourers was especially blurred. The untouchable by caste, traditionally were isolated from holding land. There was a very large body of workers and poor peasants living at the very bottom of the agarian hierachy and masses of people lived at a very low level of subsistence An average villager who dependents, on agriculture for livelihood himself and his dependents, usually remained from hand to mouth. UPs Settlement Commissioner wrote as follows about Agra district in April 1930, "In years of scarcity there must be serious underfeeding and this is bound to leave a proportion of the pouplation in no condition to resist the attack of fever or influenza.[1]

The position of agricultural labourers in the eastern most divisions of UP was quite worse. Among untouchable labourers in Basti district, it was observed in the 1950s, " the practice of eating gobraha (grains collected from animals, excreta and cleaned) is common. Almost one - fifth (1/ 5) of the population of the district is compelled to resort to these abnormal practices.

The general condition of all the UP villages presented a sad scenario. The area was more densely populated than southern or

---

1. Elizabeth White Comb, Argarian Conditions in Northern India,

cerntral India. It was less developed in terms of irrigation facilities and urban employment opportunities than the Punjab and western India. Above all the demands on the subordinate sections of agrarian society in the province were fall heavier than in other regions. The British fixed their demand first at 83 percent of the rental than 75 percent, than 66 percent. Between this was found high at last in 1858, they limited the state demand to 50 per cent of the rental. An income tax of 50 per cent on the profits of cultivation was a heavier assessment that was not known in any country being ruled by a civilized government. From 1871, a number of new taxes were assessed on land in addition to the land revenue. If the land revenue was 50 percent of the rental the total assessment on the soil including the new taxes came to 50 percent, or 58 per cent or even 60 percent of the rental. All this exposed the economic greedof the alien rulers.

Price rise was the another importnat factor responsible for tensions in rural area. It was a general assumption that a rise in prices was beneficial to the cultivator. In UP and especial in Awadh the class which had benefited from the price rise was the class of landlords, Mahajans and rich cultivators. In the province majority of small cultivator were indebted to the Mahajans and had to recduce debts at a ridiculous rate. Thus the price which the tenant got for their produce used to be thrashing price arranged by the Mahajans in the latter's interest.[1]

The rent and debt absorbed the whole produce of the cultivators. They could not use the fruits of their harvest, good or bad. The poor class of peasants and landless labourers had to purchase grain from the open market and of the most inferior quality. As such the sad plight of the poor peasants created inner discontentment.

Between 1910 and 1921 the prices of Bajra and Jawar had gone up 45 per cent, Maize and Barley by 28 per cent and Wheat by 60 per cent. High prices totally distroyed the condition of the cultivators who as a class did not get even one full meal a day and found extremely difficult to pay their rent. Thus during the

1. Pratapgarh Sett,emnt Report, 1896, p. 105.

war period, the high prices could not benefit the cultivators and brought the peasants discontent to its maximum.

The economic condition of the peasantry had become progressively worse in the winter of 1930-31 when the wheat price had reached its lowest point and the Govt. of the United Provinces had not yet implemented any measures of relief. During the period of great depression in 1930-35, there was a fall in prices all over India. The Government remissions at this time, were far from adequate and it proved to be very difficult to compel the landlords to pass on these remissioins to the peasants. On the preceding period of increasing rents and expanding credit most of the landlords had run up debts and now the money lenders at their door step and they in turn pounced on their tenants.

The peasantry of this province was exploited due to high rents as well as oppressive system of the British. They had to pay interest on loans and to pay off the debt itself. Due to this forced necessity the peasant had to grow those crops, that are called cash crops. The peasant grew more and more of those crops of which he ate less and less. This commercialization of agriculture was not a progressive step. It was a typical feature of the colonial rule. The peasants responded to the high rents by expanding their cultivation or by substituting his crops. But they could not meet the situation by increasing the productivity of his land as they had neither the security of tenure nor the necessary capital reserve. The irregularities of monsoon also increased there problems.

During the entire British rule, the peasantry of United Provinces suffered exploitation, torture and harassment. There was an alliance between alien imperialism and native imperialism which made the conditions more oppressive to the poor. Imperialism and feudalism interdependent for their existence and acted in perfect collaboration in the province of Awadh. The tenantry was exposed to an entirely hostile environment. The only reward which the peasants had in return of their toil and tears, was kicks, curses and a hungry stomach.[1] The power of monsoon over

1. Jawaharlal Nehru, An Autobiography, New Delhi. 1962, p. 52

life and powerlessness of the peasantry to change its course had become the characteristic of the rural society in U.P.

No change in basic structure of rural society could be possible because the alien rulers did not try to emancipate the Indian land from its dependence on monsoon agriculture. The rigid revenue system and the population growth left a grim mark.

There was no solace and relief for the tillers of the soil and they were left with the only option of launching a do or die movement in future.

3

Actual Events in 19th Century

Slavery came to be regarded as a curse and the people of India including the peasants hated the British. This hatred burst out in 1857 in the first revolt for freedom. They needed an opportunity and they found it when the sepoys, the chief strength of British in India, openly broke out into armed revolt against them. The revolt spread in almost all parts of Uttar Pradesh. Uttar Pradesh was the only state where the revolt developed into a mass revolt and it can rigihtly be regarded as the national way of independence. In the centenary year of the revolt in 1957, the eminent historian Dr. S.N. Sen observed, "What began as a war of religion ended as a war of independence for there is not the slighted doubt that. The rebels wanted to get rid of the alien government and restore the old order in which the King of Delhi was the rightful and representative.[1]

The Indian people began the revolt for fear of conversion and agrarian grievances. The people recognised the British as their first and last enemy and so they helped the landlords, who were also fighting against the alien rulers. A number of rural communities of UP participated in 1857 rebellion and a scene of general uprising against the British was very much evident.

The revolt of 1857 was not the first explosion of the dissatisfaction of the rural people. Many civil and rural disturbances of a serious nature occurred in the pre-mutiny and mutiny periods because these were primarily anti-British and anti-colonial movements organized throuh feudal channels. The landed chiefs in the earlier period took up arms to resist the trespass made upon their position and rigts. in the mutiny period they fought in defence of their title to the land. Throughout the first century of

1. S.N. Sen, Eighteen Fifty Seven, Calcutta, 1957, p. 411.

British rule in India, the British administration attacked on Awadh Zamindars, except those who were living in areas under permanent settlement. In North West provinces, the village system was introduced in complete reversion of the Talukdari system, and also in immediately before the mutiny secured the rights of the peasant proprietors as against the Zamindars. But the result were equally disastrous. The liquidation of the talukdars and the exaltation of the village proprietors produced a kind of social imbalance and caused grave economic dislocation which mingled with the religious discontents and fears of the mutiny period. Neither the peasant and nor the field owners of upper India were satisfied. The baffling situation indicated that the British administration could not formulate a suitable plan of land economy in which the large proprietors and village proprietors could co exist on the soil. The village landowners had many grievances to complain in respect of taxes, impoistions and imposts. Thus both in the premutiny and mutiny periods it was the class of landed chiefs who led the struggle against the British and the other classes of rural people thronged round these landed chiefs and recognised them as their natural leaders. Due to them these movements found representative character.

The political and social factors making for the Revolt of 1857 were very much interrelated. While wars and conquests led to the extermination of the Indian powers, the settlement operations which accompanied them for the adjustment of revenue and rent in the ceded and conduered provinces were proving fatal to the interests of the landed gentry of the country. Settlement and resumption were the two processes of the British revenue administration by which the aristocracay of the land was obliterated. This subversion of the supremacy of the old landlords created a grave social disorder and disaffection.

In this settlement of the North-West Provinces, the government showed favour to the inferior agricultural classes. The British challenged the titles of the landed gentry and their right and privileges allowed to them by the former government. According to the British theory of land tenure, the proprietorship of the soil was taken as vested in the cultivators, and the so-called proprietors were regarded merely as agents through whom the rents of the cultivators were to be paid to the government. The goverment justified its policy on the ground that in this part of the country, the proprietary rights of single families and village communities survived in more recognisable forms than anywhere else. Thus the talukdars or owners of group of villages were deprived of their estates which in many cases they held for ages.

In the fifties of the nineteenth century the British in India gave the impression of a faithless people whose only principle seemed to be to seize everything of value that fall within their grasp. The plundering of kingdoms and the absorption of vast estates were carried on with impunity. But this behaviour of the British loosened their hold on the Indians more than anything else and specially on the peasantry.

The sale of real property in execution of decrees issued by the British courts which reduced the families to ruin was a potent factor in producing social restiveness in the period immediately preceding. The bigger propritors as well as the peasants were hard hit. Every year large numbers of estates were put upto sale under the decrees of the Courts in satisfaction of arrears of revenue and sometimes even for simple contract debts. The sale of land not merely uprooted the ordinary people from their small holdings but also destroyed the gentry of the provinces and both the orders being the victims of the operation of British civil law were united in the revolutionary epoch of 1857-58 in a common effort to recover what they had lost.

The vast uprising of 1857 had more than one source of its origin. The sepoys revolted because they sincerely believed that their religion was in danger. The political and economic motives were also important. There was a sense of degradation so natural due to the domination of a foreign race. The grievances under which the population laboured, the hatred of the British amongst the higher classes, the fears and anxieties of the lower classes, the restiveness of the pre-mutiny period were all responsible for the disturbances of the pre-mutiny period were all responsible for the outburst of the revolt. The materials of disaffection, produced by long sufferigns, were ready to be ignited by the slightest spark that was lit by the sepoys of the British army on 10th May 1857 at Meerut.

Thus, the Revolt of 1857 that burst before the appointed time was not an isolted movement. Rather it contained the seeds of mass revolt who were dissatisfied with the British rule. The most important grasp in this movement were the peasants and the small landlords who were against the British rule for their own grievances.

U.P. was the chief centre where the main drama of 1857's rebellion was enacted. The north west provinces consisted of eight administrative divisions those of Banaras, Allahbad, Kanpur Jhansi. Agra, Rohilkhand, Meerut and Delhi. The conflagration started from Meerut as a sepoy mutiny and took the form of civil rebellion and the peasant struggles. The effects of sepoy mutiny started form Meerut were quickly felt in the whole on north-west provinces and specially in Doab which became the scene of continuous disturbances. These uprisings differed in nature and dimension to local conditions and ofther pressures yet in type and pattern these were much the same. The infection of civil rebellion which spread over the whole of upper india had a more significant character than the violence committed by the sepoys.

In Muzaffarnagar, a station about midway between Saharanpur and Meerut, civil rebellion that broke out preceded the mutiny. An explosion occurred at Muzaffarnagar in 14 May. The people plundered the tahsils, bungalows and destroyed the jail and killed the Baniyas and Mahajans. In September the rebellion in the district became so general that the local government maintained only a mere existence and its officers were put to the sword. Initial reverses of the British troops from the Kandhla pargana, turned the rising into a vast upsurge of the people of several villages of the south-western part of the tehsil.[1]

1. Narrative of Events inthe merrut Division by commissioner F. Williams, pp. 204 - 11

In Saharnpur peasants belonging to gujar and ranghar community broke out on the news of Meerut outbreak. They robbed the bankers and money lenders and plundered the police-stations and thasils. Marao Singh the head man of the village of Manakpur in Mangalpur tahsil declared himself the Raja and imposed taxes on the people. But he failed in the long run.

At Aligarh district, a brahman named Narayana belonging to a neighbouring village of Aligarh was found tempering with the loyalty of the sepoys on 20 May. He was hanged in the evening of the same day and suddenly the army broke out. Though the British recovered the station on 29 May, rebellion reged all throughout the district for long and upset the British administration.

The Rajputs combined with the Jats plundered the villages. Rao Bhopal Singh of Khair, at the head of his Chauhan followers proclaimed a Rajput government but was attacked and executed. The whole village stood in arms and challenged the British.[1]

In Agra division the outbreak of rural people came to be seen in a high revolutionary spirit. One Rang Bahadur committed excesses towards the end of June. Darbar Singh set himself as an independent Raja in the south of the district and beigan to collect revenue. Durjan Singh a brother of Tej Singh the Raja of Mainpuri, came with five hundred followers in the middle of August and burnt Manikpur. Many other leaders rose up against the British, usurped power and enforced the collection of revenue.

On the western side of Agra district, specially the Kasganj area was turned into a strong centre of the rebel.

In Mathura, the revolt started by the 44th and 67th regiments on 30 May 1857, which was continued by the villagers who jumped bravely in the movement. It appeared as if the whole country arose almost simultaneously. When the Nimach mutineers entered the district of Mathura the conflagration spread far and wide, Debi Singh declared himself as Raja of fourteen villages and set up a parallel government, Anarchy was rampart in the northern and

1. R. Spankie to F. Williams, Commissioner, Meerut, 26 Sept. 1857, Para-II in Narrative of Events Regarding the Mutiny of India of 1857 - 58 p. 468.

western parts of Mathura. At Chhata some of the rebel Zamindars stubornly held out against the English but they were effecitively defeated.

The villagers achieved a victory at Firozabad. The tehsil of kheragarh in the south of Agra was completely plundered. The pargana of Pinahat fell into disorder and was usureped by the villagers headed by Lachhman Singh, the Gujar Zamindar of Khera.

In Itmadpur Zorawar Singh of Himmatpur became very powerful in this movement. He attacked the tahsil which was sacked but he was restrained as soon as the civil administration was restored.[1]

In the paragana of Fatehabad, two villages Dhanaula and Khande were in ferment, collecting ammunition and guns. Towards the end of November, Phillps the Magistrate and Major Henness led a full scale military expedition against them.[2]

In Akrabad leaders like Jayadal, Mangal Singh and government organised the villagers to fight against the Ganya Singh rose in an open rebellion in the village of Lakshmanpour and Narah.

The adjacent district of Mainpuri in the Doab was similarly affected. As the outbreak occurred, the surrounding regions were also ablaze, Raja Tej Singh who had been shorn of 3/4 of his estate by the settlement of 1840, threw himself in the movement to secure his hereditary dignity. With his levies he came to support other rebel formations against the British power in the neighboring districts and allied himself with the Nawab of Farrukhabad. He surrendered on 11 June 1858 and was removed to Benares where he lived on an allowance.

In March 1858 a deadly sturggle ensued for the recovery of Ajitmal which was near Auraiya and twently five miles from Etawah. The peasants of the neighbouring villages formed the bulk of the army and defended the place from the attacks of the English. Drastic measures were adopted and many of the villages

1. NE, 1.69.
2. NE 76-77

were burnt down. But the British troops were fiercely attacked by isolated parties of insurgents in a guerilla style. On 11 April the rebel forces drew round Ajitmal from all directions and collected together to start a tierce tight. Niranjan Singh, Ganga Singh, Pitam, Bankat and Rup Singh participated in this struggle. However, the Yamuna-Chambal Doab was re-occupied by Lieutenants Graham and Allan in September-October 1858.

The Revolt of 1857 which was not a revolt by the Nawabs, Rajas and Talukdars alone but also a war of the people spread like fire. It broke out in Farrukhabad, Shanajanpur and Badaun, the towns of Doab where the people joined in large numbers and accepted the leadership of the local Nawabs. The area was particularly agricultural and peasants were totally dissatisfied with the agrarian policy of the British. The dimensions of the people participation in the struggle of 1857 is proved by the fact that the road to Agra was totally blocked due to the peasants who left the villages and collected on the road to meet the British army. Such was their courage

In the Allahabad division more than one thousand villages and towns and having a population of more than a million, the people revolted against the British. It has been the most memorable revolt in Indian history when the peasantry and the dispossessed zamindars made a common cause and bravely plundered the areas.

In the pargana of CHID where the Mohammdan population was in majority, the people revolted under the green flag. A revolutionary urge was present among them. The reason of their discontent was their economic grievances. In Secundra village there was a clash between the ex-zamindars and the auction purchasers. The peasantry actively joined and plundered the entire region. Though the Britishers suppressed movement, yet it again spread widely in the region of Sultanpur and Phapamau. The local people again raised their flags and reconquered the territories. The Nazim of Sultanpur named Mehandi Hasan and the Naib Nazim of Salone district Raibareili held the charge of

Allahabad paragana and occupied the north region of Allahabad. These people were inspired by patriotism and adopted gurilla warfare. They knew that the English army was better equipped with arms and ammuniation and they could not face them, still they were determined to do and die. In an encounter on 14 July 1858, Brigadier Brakerly cunningly invaded the rebels and cruelly killed them. In the official dispatch frequent mentions have been made that even after this defeat Hanuman Singh and Vilait Hussain collected large number of people and boldly revolted again. Their headquarter was very close to the railway line where they could easily fortify against the British. The revolt at Allahabad inspired the peasants of Bundelkhand, Awadh, Azamgarh, Jaunpur and to some extent it influenced Bihar too.[1]

In Cawnpore (Kanpur) Baji Rao built a lagre state, ten miles away at Bithur. He died in 1851 and left his adopted son Dhundu Pant, better known as Nana Sahib. Nana tried to secure his adopted father's pension and other honours. Many courtiers like Azimullah Khan and Tantia Tope were his devoted followers. He also jumped in the movement.

The mutiny at Cawnpore broke out on the morning of 4 June when the 2nd cavalry and first regiment left their lines[2]. After that they marched to Nawabganj where they were received by Nana Sahib and fated by him.[3] The revolt of Nana Sahib gave a new turn to the mutiny of the sepoys. What began as a military insurrection gradually appeared to have merged into a social war of disaffected landlords who made the common cause with Nana to preserve the elements of their social life. The official reports make clear that in Cawnpore the civil rebellion that followed the mutinying was very extensive in character. Bithur, Jajamau, Sheorajpur, Narwal and Rasulabad were the main centres of the revolt. In Bithur almost all the Chaudhuries and Zamindars were influeced by Nana Sahib. They were Chuni Singh, Bahadur Singh, Muni Singh and Kishori

1. Hindu Patroit, 29 July, 1858, Malltson, Ill, 280.
2. NE, i. pp.
3. Report by CB. Thomhill, Commissioner

Singh who turned rebels. About the 10th of July Nana Sahab had more than twenty thousand armed fighting men of all classes including peasants and zamindars[1]. But according to the native sources the number of Zamindars and armed peasants, followed that Nana Sahib was more than 58,000 men. All the twenty six villages of Chauhan Rajputs and twelve villages of Daria Singh Zamindar fought in the revolt with hundred of peasants and their sub chiefs in favour of Nana Sahib on 27th November, 1857, the rebel leaders of Cawnpore and Kalpi defeated the British.[2]

People of Fatehpur revolted against the British although it was not a military station. Zamindars of this area prepared themselves and the peasants attacked on treasury on 8 June. They destroyed the mission premises and the bungalows of the British. After these incidents, the Europeans, left the station. Disaffected peasants, villagers hunted out auction purchasers and decree holders and attacked them in revengeful mood.

The Rohilkhand division consisted of five administrative districts, Bareilly, Moradabad Shahjanpur, Budaun and Bijnour. It had an area of 1880 miles and a population of nearly 700,000 people. The Muslim population in this area was strong both in number and in influence. In Rohilkhand the revolt was mostly directed by the Muslim community which hated immensly the British. However it was not limited only the muslims. The rising was of a popular character when both the Hindus and the Muslims fought collectively to end the British rule.

There was a spontaneous uprising in Bijnor when the people started moving together and taking part in the movement. The disaffected gujars swarmed all along the Ganges, the banjaras On the north, the Mewatis on the Moradabad border and the Jats and Chauhans in other parts. Mohammad Khan, the nawab of Najibabad established an independent government after the withdrawal of the British army. But he could not restore law and order. The conflict in the country continued till 21 April 1858,

1. Chick, the Annals of the Indian Rebellion, 820
2. Chick, op. cit, 618

when Jones achieved a powerful victory on a huge rebel force comprising one thousand infantry and two thousand cavalry.[1]

In Moradabad district landed chief, peasants and other people participated in the revolt. The principal station in Rohilkhand was Bareilly where the Mahomedans followed the challenging current. A large number of disaffected civil population took part in the rebellion of Shahjanpur. In the interior parts of Shahjahanpur peasants of the adjoining villages broke out into open rebellion. Tehsils were plundered, records were destroyed and police stations were burnt. People of neighbouring villages destroyed sugar refinery and wine factory.[2]

In Fyzabad division the sepoys broke out in revolt when they plundered the treasury and opened the jails.

Talukdars and landlords of Fyzabad, especially the Palwars of Bihar, the Bajhgot of Hasanpur, joined the rebellion in large numbers. Udit Narain Singh, a Zamindar of Birhar and a Palwar Chief plundered the pugitives from Fyzabad at Narani in the Birhar pargana. Madho Prasad, Pradas Singh was another Birhar talukdar. He was friendly to British in the early stages but subsequently he also rose in arms and excited other chief of the nieghbouring places like Kishan Prasad, Sheo Prakash and Raja Prithipal Singh to join the revolt. Prithvi Pal Singh collected a large force and took possession of all the villages of which he had been deprived of by the government in the districts of Sultanpur and Pratapgarh.

In the region of Awadh the civil rebellion took the form of a Talukdari movement. The landlord class took advantage of the situation for the recovery of their lost estates. In some cases they also revolted against the alien government, but in general their attention was confined to the reversal of British land settlement which was against their personal interests.

Sitapur the north west division of Awadh also revolted and the rising was general nature. The Nazim of Khairabad, Bakshi,

1. NE, 518 Report by Major H. Ramsay Commissioner of Kumaon.
2. NE i, 444, J.W. Kaye, A History of the Sepoy war in India (1880), iii p-279

Harprasd represented the civil war, a leader Khanali Khan collected a force of three thousand men and fought bravely.[1]

In Barabanki, the landlords with an army of 15 thousand men fought with the British at Nawabganjon, the Fyzabad road eighteen miles beyond Lucknow. They fought heroically, Brigadier Hope Grant and Leiutent Majendie occupied Nawabganj on 14 June 1858, and the revolt was crushed. In Unnao Havelock's forces had to fight with the peasants, who gave a strong resistance.

The rising at Lucknow can be called as the central event of the rebellion. On 27 May 1857, Mahomedans of Malihabad revolted and gave a tough fight. The angry peasants armed themselves and they were watching the actions of the British when the infantry regiment broke out.[2] The sepoy rebels created great excitement among the people. Captain Anderson who was Assistant Commissioner at Lucknow heard of it and became prepared to face them.[3]

The whole of Awadh passed out of the hands of the British. Villagers followed the examples of the towns, helped the mutineers to sustain their struggle. On 30 June 1857, the British forces were defeated at the hands of the Indians at Chinhat, a village on the Fyzabad road.

The Mutiny at Lucknow merged in the war of tlukdars. They either joined the rebel forces or sent their men to fight against the British in a large numbers Forbes Mitchel said that it needed no great powers of observation to fully understand that the whole population of Awadh against us."

By the end of December 1858, the British reconquered the whole of Awadh after defeating native forces in different wars. The risings in Gorakhpur division were the same in nature as in Awadh. The landlords or talukdars took part in the rebellion for reconquering their lost estates. They were discontented because

1. Incidents in the Sepoy War, 267.
2. Anderson, Apersonal Journal of the siefe of Lucknow, 9-11
3. Rees, A Personal Narrative, 21-26

of the summary settlement of the land revenue. The peasants were under their influences and so they fought boldly on their side.

In Benaras division there was a scene of a country wide resurgence. The old Zamindars were disaffected and had relations with the disaffected talukdars of Awadh.

In Jhansi division the revolt of sepoys was preceded by a vast upsurge of the people. The jail prisoners who were released at Allahabad excited the people and they began indulge in fury and bloodshed. The presents of the tahsil of Manu rose together and attacked the police thana and tahsil and their amla. They distroyed the government properly. A treasury containing rupees one thousand and two hundred was plundered. The official records were burst and distributed to the winds. The people of Banda and the peasants of neighbouring villages in the tahsil of Pailani rose in arms. The Mohamedan peasants of the village Chilla were the most aggressive in the revolt.[1]

Nawab Ali was a great leader who was faithful to the British but later joined the war against them. The rebellion found dimensions and spread to other parts. The whole region of Banda revoted and the neighbouring districts of Fatehpur, Allahabad, Hamripur were all in the hands of insurgents. The peasantry of the area rose in revolts in every direction. The revolution was more rapid and and more complete in Banda than in any other area.[2]

On 14 June, when the British officers left Banda, Nawab Ali established his own rule. On 29 September, when Kunwar Singh with two thousand men reached Banda, he was received with great honour and hospitality by the Nawab. He stayed there for some time and then went towards Kalpi.[3]

Thus the rebellious peoloe were in an aggerssive mood. The British power oocupied Banda on 15 February, 1858 after defeating them.

The popular character of the rebellion at Banda reflected in

1. NE, 521. Report of F.P. Mayne Magistrate and Collector.
2. NE, 528
3. NE, 531-32

the activities of rural masses. The official reports tell that there was the activities of rural masses. The official reports tell that there was not a single village that had not involved in the anti-British activities. The rebellion spread from village to village. Many villages remained in open rebellion for a long time.

In Hamirpur district a general uprising followed the mutiny when people rose in all sides and attacked the bankers of the money lenders, peasants and specially the actual purchasers, who had gained possession of half the estate in the distric. In Hamirpur, an inevitable war between ex-zamindars and actual purchasers became inevitable.[1] In July 1857 Nana Saheb established his rule in most of the villages of Hamirpur.

In Jalaun district, the villagers had not shown much interest in the early period of revolt but later several militant leaders sprang up from among them. Barjor Singh, a rabel Rajput plundered Kunch, Ganbhi Singh and Debi Singh raided Mote, a tehsil station on the Kalpi road, thirty five miles from Jhansi. At that time the British were busy in the sturggle with Sindhia in Gwalior and Jaloun practically fell in to the hands of Barjar Singh and Daulat Singh.

The soldiers struck the first blow of the great Revolt of 1857, Their grievances flowed independently on any external pressure and orginated from the conditions of the existing military service. But their fears about the intentions of the British to destroy their caste and religion were exactly those which also troubled the minds of the civil population, whether urban or rural and the feudal aristocracy as well. The soldiers had no plan and resources either, and in many cases, they sought the help of the landed dignitaries. After the explosion at Meerut the mutinus troops went to Delhi were Bahadur Shah, the last Muslim emperor lived. By adopting him as leader the Indian legitimists gave the movement a traditional countrywide base and acceptance of civil population. The military revolt in fact took a form of civil revolt and villages, peasants, landlords took part and fought against the British. A

1. Chick, op. Cit, 510

rumour that the British power was gone unsettled the minds of the people and the British faced a really national and revolutionary situation growing out of the Meerut event.

The most immediate factor which inspired peasantry to break out and sacrifice their lives was the religious element. "Their religion was in danger" had been the most inspiring feeling that inspired people to do and die for their caste and creed.

The religious feeling mingled with the racial issue. The British had a universal hatred for Indians. It gave a national colouring to the revolt of 1857. The people decided to tear the English out of the land root and branch. The peasantry of U.P. in general was actually in sympathy with the rebels. The selfless spirit which was seen in different places confirms it. The most remarkable and dignified fact was that the villagers did not betray their rebel leaders. On the contrary the rebels were helped by the villagers. There was a strong feeling of patriotism in the hearts of rural masses of North-West Provinces and Awadh.

When it was recognised that the mutiny of the sepoys had been turned into a civil rebellion, the government passed an act to punish the person guilty of rebellion with death. The law was further extended by the act XIV passed on 6 June 1857 by which provision was made for capital punishment of persons convicted of exciting mutiny or sedition. Act XVI, XVII and Act XXV of 1857 were passed to meet the challenge given to the government from the civil populace. Other several measures were also adopted. Even burning of offending villages was considered a necessity where the peasantry had committed a grave outrage. Indiscriminate slaughter of men, burning the whole villages, blowingh up of rebels by hundreds became their routine many villages were burnt down and for miles dead bodies hung from trees.[1] R.H. Danlop's punitive forces first killed all the males and then burnt down the villages of Akulpur and Busoundm Meerut.[2]

In Arrah, the wholesale burning and destruction of all villages

1. Kaye II, 604-6. Majendie, UP Among the Pandies, 224-26.
2. FP, IX, 886-8

was recommended by the British.[1] Same incidents happened in the villages of Jaunpur. Colonel Forster while moving on to Porhat distroyed over thirty villages and seized all the grain stored there.

These incidents proved that the Revolt of 1857 was not an isolated revolt. The people specially the peasantry of the provinces joined it in overwhelming numbers. Canning represented to the Court of Directors that the undue action of the civil authorities could not be checked - crucial hangings and burning and plunder of villages proved that the government created a general bloody prosecution which was largely condemned.

The mutiny which at the beginning was little more than a military revolt infact grew fast into a wide spread fire. The agricultural classes and, their civil rulers together to free the country from the cruel and exploitative British. The tatukdars and landlords dominated the rebellion but they made it possible only by the co-operation of the villagers of the different social status. In Awadh the British were facing not only a mutiny, but fighting revolt of peasants under their hereditary chiefs and leaders. In Budaun the rural elements rose in a body and continued the rebellion after the sepoys had left. In Mathura the whole country had risen immediately after the great outbreak. In Allahabad the peasatry rose at once under their old talukdars.[2] This prompt attitude of the people was indeed commendable.

Thus, 1857 can be regarded as the first start of peasant movements in UP. Although they were not well organised and did not have very competent leadership, yet they fought heroically and even showed capacity for co-ordinated action. In Allahabad, the character of rural risings was such that it could not have been any the stronger and more formidable event if it had been skilfully planned and deliberately matured. The peasantry was not only opposed the British but they were opposing every kind of exploitation of the British. In Saharanpur the rebels destroyed the Bania houses and threw the accounts into the flames. The same

1. The Hindu Patriot, 8 July 1858
2. The Hindu Patriot, 8 July 1858

thing happened at Mathura[1]. In whole of the Provinces the rising of the sepoys and people were almost simultaneous in point of time, and the alliance between the millitary and agricultural classes was the closest of its kind.

The revolt was the first combined attempt of many classes of people to challenge the alien rulers in which the peasants of UP participated with full energy and strength. The Doab region, between the Ganges and Jamuna was the chief center of these peasant disturbances. The events of the revolt were such that it became very easy to clear the process by which military mutiny was converted into a peasant rebellion. Some of the key features of this process was the capture of key urban centres by the mutiners, the autonomous peasant uprising in the country side and the linking of the two by political leadership supplied from the magnate classes. How adventurous it was to celebrate the centenary of the battle of Palasi with blood and tears over an extensive. It was in fact, the beginnigs of the end of British power in India.

1. Kaye ii, 260

4

Stray Events in 20th. Century

The peasant movement in 20th century had such distinctive features as constitute a major landmark in the development of agitation against British rule. Ultimately these agitations were merged in the nationwide struggle for freedom. The peasant movement which began in 1920 became sychronous with the non cooperation movement and the peasant compaigns of 1930's were inspired by civil disobedience movement.

The peasant movements of U.P. had certain distintive aspects of their own. They had their own class character, leadership, organizations, ideology and the historical background. The orgainzations of kisan sabha helped the peasant to be united and gave them effective leadership and the guidelines. The high ideals and character of peasant leaders greatly inspired them. Baba Ram Chandra was the chief inspiring personality to the peasants of Awadh. The struggle was against the exploitation of both the landlords and the alien rulers. In this sense the 20th century peasant agitaiton was the conflicts which had already begun during the 19th century.

From the pre-British days talukdars had remained the most dominant landed class in Awadh. In the later Mughal period they were only rent collecting intermediaries between the Nawab and the actual cultivators, the Kisans. The weaknesses of Nawab's rule had encouraged them to build estates and to acquire the quasi-independent political estates. At first the British considered the talukdars as a reactionary body and recognise them as an oppressive social class that stood in the way of rapid agricultural Improvement. During the out break of the revolt of 1857, the large scale participation of the Awadh talukdars in the revolt with the support of the villagers, changed the British attitude. They began to accept the strength of the talukdars in the social structure of rural Awadh. The government changed its policy towards them and changed its towards them and recognised them as the "Natural Leaders" of the people.[1]

After the outbreak of the Rrevolt of 1857, the British authorities adopted the protective policy and looked after the interest of the talukdars. The talukdars also gave their loyalty and support to the government. Their loyalty continue till the end of the Raj. The Talukdar class gradually lost the political strength and what they enjoyed was only the economic luxuries. They had abandoned their self-respest and independence and become the mere shadow of the alien colonial government. They exploited the poor peasantry to fulfil the demands of the aliens. The double exploitation inspired the peasantry to be organized and to struggle against the oppressors.

Around 1921 the agrarian class structure in Awadh was of a complex nature. It may be classified in three broad categories of 'rent receivers' 'rent payers' and 'agricultural labour'. This was the time when Indian National Congress had become an effective body in rural areas due to the emergence of Mahatma Gandhi. From 1885 to 1900 the Indian National Congress was dominated by the urban middle class. Most of its members were nominated from Awadh for the legislative council from 1898 to 1900, and they were the talukdars and the Zamindars. The British had made them the owners of the land and they had become the masters of the large tract of cultivated land, forests and irrigational schemes. The majority of the tillers of the soil were reduced to the position of serfs or tenants without any rights. They were left to the mercy of landlords and the cruel money lenders who always exploited them.[2]

1. P. D. Reeves, Landlord and Party Politics in the United Provinces 1934-37, in D.A. Low (ed.) Soundings in the Modern South Asian History, Barkeley 1969, p.62
2. Sukhbeer Chaudhary, Peasants' and Workers' Movement in India (1905-22) p.22

According to the U.P. Banking Enquiry Committee Report, " In the United Provinces the total indebtedness upto 1930 was about Rs. 125 corers as such."[1] The province was in the condition of bitter poverty and bankruptcy. In the post war years the wages of the agricultural workers fluctuated between 1.5 and 4 annas a day, whereas in Punjab a day's usual wages were 12 annas.[2]

The bitter poverty was due to the dual exploitation. By the British on the one hand and the landlords and talukdars on the other. Referring to their chacacters Pt. Jawaharlal Nehru wrote," The talukdars and the big zamindars, the lords of the land , the Natural leaders of the people," as they are proud of calling themselves, have been the spoilt children of the British governments.

The landlords were actually the parasites on the land and the people. Their chief activity lay in endeavouring to placate the local officials, without whose favour they could not exist for long. They demanded ceaselessly a protection of their own special interest and priviledges. They did not have even the virtues of an aristocracy. As a class they were morally and itellectually degenerate. They had out lived their day Nehru prophesied that they would survive till the British government props them up.[3]

In his telegram sent to the Secretary of State for India in January 1921, the viceroy recognised that the "Tenancy Act favouring the interests of Talukdars admittedly needed amendment and that genuine discontent of the tenants with the working to the existing laws was the main reason for the success attained by the non-cooperators."

In the summary report of the peasant disturbances prepared by the Government of India in the light of the informantions provided by the U.P. Government it was admitted that the "Agrarian population had legitimate grievances. The government pointed out that the difficulties are social and economic rather that

1. Ibid; p. 75-76
2. Documents of Royal Commission on Agriculture in India Vol -1, 1935
3. Jawahar lal Nehru, An Autobiography, Allied Publishers, New Delhi, 1962, p. 68

political they began considering the proposals for the amendment of Awadh rent Act[1].

There were no alternatives for government service except agriculture. The deplorable condition of unemployment and poverty caused the conditon of starvation. Terrible epidemics spread like wild fire and turned the province into a peramanent breeding ground of drought and disease. The famine of 1920-21 caused further deterioration in the situation.[2]

Organization of Kisan Sabhas

The peasantry of the provinces was utterly tired of its economic and social ailments. They were fed up with the exploitation and tortures. The discontent grew deeper at the dawn of the twentieth century. In 1917, some peasant thought of a peasant organization competent enough to fight for their genuine demands.

In 1918, a U.P. Kisan Sabha was formed at Allahabad by some nationalist leaders, who were participating in the home rule movement. Sir Purushottam Das Tondon became its president and Indra Narain Dwivedi was appointed its secretary. The second annual meeting of U.P. Kisan Sabha was held at Prayag on 31 January 1919. Ram Nath Tripathi was in the chair during the third and fourth meetings of this organization.

These meeting and deliberations held at Allahabad on 21 January 1920 and on 7th February.[3] due to the non cooperation proposal of the Indian National Congress and many other matters created differences between Sri Purushottam Das Tondon and Pt. Jawaharlal Nehru on one side and Indra Narain Dwivedi on the other. As a result the U.P. Kisan Sabha was split in the two groups.[4]

---

1. Disturbances in the Rae Bareilly and Faizabad districts Home (Pol.) department proceedings February, 1921 file no 195-216 p.10
2. A.M. Dyakov(ed.) A contemporary History of Inidan Peoples, Publishing House New Delhi. 1964, p. 79
3. Mazid Hayat Siddiqui, Agrarian Unrest in North India, The United Provinces 1918-22, p. 123
4. Abhudya (Weekly Allahabad) 13 August, 27August 1921.

One Kisan Sabha was estabished by the peasant themselves in which Jningury Singh and Sahdev Singh took up the leadership. It was in village Rure of Patti tehsil in Pratapgarh district in 1920.[1] This Sabha became the mouth piece and gave birth to a mass movement. Through this organization of their own, the peasants could voice their demands and grievances and could reside the Talukdars exploitation.

The U.P. Kisan Sabha established in 1918 also began to spread out by June 1919 at least 450 branches of U.P. Kisan Sabha had been formed in 173 tahsils of United Provinces."

Political awareness of home rule league which was organized by some of the educated lawyers on the contrary the Awadh Kisan Sabha formed at Rure was truly a peasant's body. The U.P. Kisan Sabha on the whole worked for the protection of the landed class and many of its members belonged to this class. In 1919 a meating of U.P. Kisan Sabha was held at Kanpur.

Since then its regular meetings were organized at Mainpury, Banares, Jaloun Rae-Bareilly, Gorakhpur and Eta districts of U.P.[2]

The U.P. Kisan Sabha adopted same programmes for both the regions of U.P. Agra and Awadh, though the tenurial conditions were not the same in both these regions. The Kisan Sabha soon gained great popularity in the districts of Agra region.[1] Due to its relationship with the Home Rule League and specialy because of Pandit Madan Mohan Malaviya. The U.P. Kishan Sabha became closer to the politics of Indian National Congress.

In 1918 the thirty third annual session of the Congress was held at Delhi. The Congress welcomed the presence of the peasant delegates. The 1919 session was held at Amritsar with Motilal Nehru in the chair, majority of the peasants attended the Amritsar session with support of Madan Mohan Malaviya and Motilal Nehru. In the draft proposal of the sabha it was requested that the

1. Mazid Hayat Siddiqui, Agrarian Unrest in North India, The United Provinces 1918-22, p. 123
2. Ibid.

Congress should adopt a resolution that, "The peasants all over India be declared actual owners of the land, they actually cultivated. The Sabha demanded agricultural produce as the peasats income and that it should be taxed like any other income."[1]

In June 1920 Baba Ramchandra led 200 tenants to Allahabad from Kanpur and Pratapgarh districts, they met Gouri Shanker Mishra and Jawaharlal Nehru. They urged the leaders for taking interest in matter of the poor tenants. Gouri Shanker was at that time Vice-President of the U.P. Kisan Sabha, Pt. Nehru showed a keen interest in their demands and made several trips to those areas. Though Pt. Nehru was not a member of Kisan Sabha, he paid frequent visits to the villages. He watched the Kisan movement growing in strength Pt. Nehru had true sympathy for the rural poor. Several times he was ashamed comparing his luxurious life with the hard life of the Indian peasants. He wrote, a new confidence came into the peasants, he walked straight with head up. His fear of the landlords, agents and the police vanished away."

The U.P. Kisan Sabha had adopted a moderate policy of prayers and petitions. It occasionally raised. Its voice to highlight the miserable conditions of the Awadh peasnats. It never attempted to mobilise the peasantry for their release from the talukdari clutches. It adopted the policy of taking peasant dalegations to the Congress sessions where the urban and middle class oriented Congress paid no real attention to the peasant grievances. The Congress leaders even objected to their exemption of delegate fee.[2]

While the U.P. Kisan Sabha was dominated by the urban intelligence the Rure Kisan Sabha Pratapgarh district successfully organize the masses of the pesants.[3]

Baba Ramchandra joined it in 1919 and soon he became its most powerful leader. By June 1920, about 500 branches of the Rure based Kisan Sabha had started functioning in various districts of U.P. Baba Ram Chandra soon came in touch with the

1. Intelligence Bureau Records; op. Cit Mazid Hayat Siddiqui, Agrarian Unrest in Northern India United Provinces pp. 127-28
2. Abhuadya, (Daily Allahabad) 25/12/1920.
3. Pt. Nehru, An Autobiography.

U.P. Kisan Sabha. The Rure Kisan Sabha coming in contact with the U.P. Kisan Sabha and meeting the national leaders speaded up its activities. It started publishing a pamphlet entitled " Kisan Pratigya" under Gouri Chander Misra, the Vice President of U.P. Kisan Sabha. In this pamphlet they exhibited their determination to oppose all kinds of exploitation, pay rents on the proper time, not to pay illegal ceases, not to work as begar (labour without payment) etc. The peasants also decided to settle their disputes through a panchayat. The urban leaders linked up with the village politics exploited the peasants discontent for their own party interests.[1] But the peasantry was not ready to accept any further exploitaion and was determined to fight against the talukdari system.

Consequently, the activitis of Kisan Sabha alarmed the talkudar class. They found it dangerous to their lives and property They were habited to a luxurious life, and they were not ready to easily leave their privileges. To counter the activites of Kisan Sabha , they launched a "Kisan Hitkari Sabha"[2]

The Talukdari class was indeed a parasite created by British government. It was used by them as reactionary power giving them privileges of a rich and comfortable life. The launching of "Kisan Hitkari Sabha" was a combined attempt to talukdars and British Government to combat the Kisan Movement. But the attempt failed and cannot evoked any response among the tenantry.[3]

During the first half of 1920 the Kisan Sabha meetings were held in a number of villages. On October 17 the meeting was held at Pratapgarh. It was attended by the heads of various Kisan Sabha. The agenda was to consider the question of forming a central organization of all the Kisan Sabha. Pt. Jawahar Lal Nehru was also a participant in this meeting. The meeting resolved to form the Awadh Kisan Sabha. A constitutions was formed with the assistance of Pt. Nehru. The members of this

1. Kapil Kumar, Peasant in Revolt p.48.
2. Independent, 14/9/1920.
3. Leader, Allahabad 25/9/1920

sabha decided to oppose the illegal demands of the talukdars as paying Nazranas and ejectment etc. They began to decide their disputes through panchayats and the participnts agreed to it. The formation of Awadh Kisan Sabha was a laudable achievement of the congress men. They had an organization through which they could intruduce to the peasants the principles and polices of the Congress. The Congress could influence the peasants to pursue the non cooperation programmes in big masses.

After the formation of Awadh Kisan Sabha, there was a rapid increase in the number of the local level Kisan Sabhas. By the end of October 1920 the Awadh Kisan Sabha had established over 330 Kisan Sabhas. In the Rae-Bareilly district a Kisan Sabha was formd at Rusulpur village after the visit of Baba Ram Chandra. Baba Ram Chandra also pleaded for Swadesis, Hindu Muslim Unity, and the non-cooperation movement. From Rae Bareilly, the Awadh Kisan Sabha spread to Sultanpur and Faizabad districts as well as to the entire Awadh region.[1]

Outbursts in Some Districts (1921-22)

When Kisan Sabha was busy in organizing its meetings and trying to bring their issues on political scene through the Congress, threre was something burning inside. The external peace was lull before the storm. Nehru's enquiries showed that the agrarian upheavals burst forth in their extremes. The peasants were "desperate and were quite angry and was needed to kindle the flame."[2]

The 1920 was the year when new awareness emerged among the peasantry. They wanted to end up the atrocities of the landlords. In 1921 many agrarian disturbances broke out, particularly in the Awadh region of United Provinces.

The riots spread over three districts and it started from Rae-Bareilly. The foundation of the coming struggle was laid down by an ordinary peasant who slapped a Talukdar for being immoral in his conduct towards his wife. Pt. Nehru considered this incident as

1. Leader Allahabad 31 October 1920.
2. Pt. Jawaharlal Nehru, An Autobiographyp. 57.

a starting of violence among the non-violent peasants and he was surprised on this sudden change.[1]

Such assaults on the landlords gave a new confidence to the peasants and they realized that there is no need to show false regards, the peasantry started to be united against the government, the landlords and the talukdars, the peasants began to travel without tickets in the trains, specially when they went to join a Kisan rally, orgainzed by Baba Ram Chandra at Ayodhya on 20th December 1920. The rally became a symbol of peasants, unity.[2] They perfectly knew that the crisis came to a head towards the end of 1920, when a few peasant leaders were arrested for some minor offences, they were arrested on 28th August 1920 while addressing a sabha at Lokrawan Bag in the estate of a lady talukdar Chabiraj Kunwar.[3] According to Baba Ram Cahandra about 80,000 peasant were present at the sabha to protest against a person being falesely involved in a theft case on the occasion to trial a huge gathering of the peasants filled the court compound. The Pratapgarh district Magistrate thought it dangerous to postpone the trial to the next day because the crowd went on increasing and they besieged the prison. So he ordered to free the peasant leaders.[4] Accodrding to Pt. Nehru "This was big triupmh of the peasants. And they began to think that they could always have their way by weight of numbers alone.[5] In the beginning of January 1921 the peasant revolted suddenly against their talukdars in the south of the Rae Bareilly district. A large crowd of the villagers in several thousand numbers was on the rampage in tehsil Dalmai destroyed the personal cultivation called sirland of the talukdars.

On January 1921 the crops of a talukdar Sardar Nihal Singh destroyed at Awadh village, he acuquired these vast landed interests by his suspecious role in the great revolt of 1857.[6]

1. Ibid; p.59.
2. Kapil Kumar , 'Peasant in Revolt' P. 117
3. M. H. Siddiqui, Agrarian Unrest in North India, The United Provinces p. 130-131,
4. Ibid; p.131
5. Ibid;
6. Disturbances in Rae Bareilly and Faizabad districts File No-17 p. 11

On 3 January 1921, the cropos owned by another traitor talukdar Thakur Ram Pratap Singh were destroyed in the village of Chichauli.[1] On 4th January another farm at the same place of the same talukdar were totally destroyed.[2]

On 5th January 1921 a crowd of about 1000 peasants attacked Roopchand cloth merchant and a hunch man of a lady talukdar Thakurain Shivraj Kunwar. They looted her textile merchandise in the Rustampur bazar and also took away other kinds of property.[3] In Chandaria village, Baba Janki Das guided the peasants and they surrounded the zamindar Tribhuvan Bahadur Singh.The police however somehow could save him. The police arrested thirteen peasants and Baba Janki Das. Some thing conspired between the police and the Talukdar and Baba Janki Das was charged of stealing the gold ornaments of the talukdar. He was sent to Lukcnow Jail.[4]

On 6th January 1921, the store of Sardar Nihal Singh was destroyd. The property of Raja of Tiloi was looted. A crowd of about 150 peasants looted the bazar of Mau. About 200 men looted the houses of two money lenders,[5] Badri Bania and Mussammat Durajya.

All these events proved that the peasants were fully aware of their enemies and understood the aim of their attack who were the Zamindars, Sahukqrs and the government, responsible for their grievances. The peasnats were shouting slogans in the court and the Magistrate reported that they sought inspiration from Gandhi Ji.[6]

---

1. Sukhbeer Chaudhary, 'Peasants and workers' Movements in Indian (1905-22) p. 29
2. Ibid;
3. Ibid;
4. Independent, (Weekly) Allahabad January 1921
5. Sikhbeer Chaudhary, Peasants and Workers Movement in India (1905-22) p.80
6. Telegram No. 21-F datted Lucknow 7th January 1921, from the Chief Secretary to Government of the United Provinces home (ed.) Department No. 17 p. 8.

The peasant movemnet of the Rae Bareilly district was mainly due to economic grievances. The movement reached its climax when the police opened fire on the innocent peasants at Munshiganj bridge on the outskirts or the Rae Bareilly town. Many of the peasants were arrested.[1] The news of the arrest of peasant leaders spread like wild fire, about 650 peasant went to jail voluntarily, just to see their leaders who had been departed to Lucknow jail.

The peasats were confused about the fate of the arrested leaders, some of them thought that Baba Ramchandra had been arrested and they gathered at Lucknow to get him released, some of them thought that Mahatma Gandhi had been taken in to custody.[2] The police used force and opened fire on the peasants. Many of the peasants were wounded and a few of them were killed.

The peasants retaliated with stores, lathis in which several police men were injured. Pt. Nehru also reached there. He held a meeting of the peasants and tried to Government of United Provinces, reported to the secretary of remove their fear. G.B. Lambert, the Chief Secretary to the the Government of India Home Department of 9th January 1921.

"The southern portion of the Rae Bareilly district was in a very disturbed state and rapidly going to the condition of anarchy. Serious crimes amounting to dacoity began to occur in alarming numbers.[3]"

The Secretary of state for India was greatly alarmed on these disturbances and he wired to the Viceroy on 12th January 1921, "yesterday's and today's newspapers are full of accounts with score headlines and terrific posters of agrarian riots in Rae Bareilly and Sultanpur districts beginning apparently from January 4th. It is stated that the trouble is spreading, that civil and police authorities are quite unable to handle it. The rioters have a certain amount of justice in their cause and that the suppression by land owners

1. United Provinces Legislative Council Proceedings 1921, vol 5, p.24
2. Kapil Kumar, 'Peasant in Revolt' P. 128
3. Telegram No. 17, 4E dated 9 January 1921 Proceeding Home Deartment (Pol.) (Telegram by the chief secretary of U.P.)

of "Soviets" one of the reasons for thess disturbances.[1] Please telegraph on account of these incidents." He also enquired as to how much Gandhi was connected with these riots.[2]

On 13th January, in his repling telegram the Viceroy explained that the movement was led by the people involved in non-cooperation movement and he further stated that it was not certain that Gandhi directed or guided the movement.[3]

The Secretary of state was worired about the riots to be spread in all Awadh area. On 18th January 1921, he dispatched another telegram to the vicerroy, in which he stated that, He had never heard about the existence of the "Soviets" referred in the repart telegraph.[4]

Faizabad District

On 13th and 14th January 1921, the peasants frustration in the Baskhari and Jehagirganj in Tanda tehsil of Faizabad district. The majority of villages were under the cruel Zamindars in this part of Awadh. The Kisan Sabha Movement was very well organized in this area. Most of the members and supporters of Kisan Sabha were the small tenants and low caste landless labours working in the land holding of the Brahmins.[5] On 12 January 1921, the Kisan Sabha held a meeting in which they decided not to work for the old wages. The Kisan Sabha inspired them to go on strike. They were told that the British Raj was coming to an end and Gandhian Raj was about to come and it was the wish of Mahatma Gandhi that they should oppose the landlords and not pay the taxes to them.[6]

Pt. Nehru criticized the policy of exciting the poor and ignorant peasants. Getting the idea they readily and willingly looted the

1. "Soviets" communist Institutions established among the revolutionaries affected by russian Revolution of 1917.
2. Preceddeding Home Department (Poli.) File No. 17, 1921
3. Ibid;
4. Sukhbeer Chaudhary ," Peasants and workers " Movement in India (1905-22) p. 85
5. Sukhbeer Chaudhary, Opcit. P. 85
6. Home (Pol.) Department , file No. 17,1921, p. 20

property of landlords and zamindars and shouted the slogans of "Mahatma Gandhi ki Jai", although Nehru criticized the misuse of the name of Mahatma Gandhi but he liked the revolt as it was a symbol of awareness in the oppressed and exploited classes. Looting was a process form whcih they could express their anger and frustration.

The success in their first effort inspired the peasants for further action. On 13 January the groups of lower tenants labourers were also involved in the violence. The zamindars could not offer any resistance as the peasantry came in overwhelming numbers.[1] Each group consisted of about five thousand men[2]. They attacked both petty zamindars and their allied tenants, destroyed their crops and property, looted bazars, paritcularly shops, owned by some notorious coton and grain merchants and money lenders. The Police arrested about 346 peasants.[3]

On 19th January 1921, a Zamindar punished two peasant leaders, taking revenge of the agrarian violence and loot of his family. The peasants organized meetings at Baskhari and Akbarpur on 20th and 27th January on wards. Just after these meetings there occurred a riot at the Goshaiganj where 13 peasants were arrested. A number of papers relating, to the leaders of the kisan sabha were recoverd. These contained petitions to Mahatma Gandhi relating to agrarian grievances.[4]

On 17th January 1921 the Chief Secretary to the Government of the United provinces sent the following dispatch to the Home Secretary "The agrarian position in Awadh is still uncertain. The early revision of the Awadh Rent Act is necessary."[5] The English bureaucrats adopted several measures to crush the uprisings. They presented the whole of the movement in a negative form and took severe punitive measures to demoralize the peasants. The

1. Proceeding Home Depatment (Pol.) file no. 17, 1921
2. Sukhbeer Chaudhary , " Peasants' and workers' Movement in India (1905-22) M p. 86
3. Ibid, P.87
4. Home (Pol.) Department file no. 17 1921, p.19
5. Ibid;

authorities presented the movement as the incidents of plunder and loot of different groups of "dacoits". They denied the fact that the dacoits attacked only the landlords and merchants and majority of agrarian population supported these "dacoits".[1]

Peasant Disturbances in Sultanpur District

In March 1921, another peasant disturbance broke out in Sultanpur. The British rulers did not take any interest in the peasant grievances and adopted a policy of repression. The authorities arrested the peasant and tortured them in different ways. They were beaten, assaulted, and harassed in a totally uncivilized manner by a government belonging a race that was called civilized. The newspaper entitled "Independent" published from Allahabad wrote in its editorial that "The oppression is so great when a person is arrested, he is mercilessly beaten until he is senseless or unless he promises to make his statement just as the police desired Rae Bareilly was the district which played the most glorious part in the peasant movement. The area further glorifed itself in the fire of revolution on 20th March 1921. The disturbance started from Salon tehsil of Rae Bareilly. The peasant leaders decided to held a large Kisan meeting at Karpai in Salon tehsil. On the day when the meeting was organizing, the police attacked them and tried to arrest the two peasant leaders Brij Pal Singh and Jhanku Singh. In the protest the assembled peasants counter attacked the police and forced them to run away.[2]

Another police force arrived with the Superintendent of Police. The crowd assembled there numbered about several thousand strong peasants. The police tried to disperse it, but nobody moved. They were shouting the slogans like "Mahatma Gandhi ki Jai". This went on all the night. The peasants were waiting for Mahatama Gandhi to come there. Many of them were armed with the spears. However the police, eventually succeeded in suppressing them. Brijpal Singh was arrested when they tried to arrest Janku Singh, he protested and called crowd to save him.

1. Independent (Daily) Allahabad 6th March 1921
2. Ibid

The crowd followed him, made a rush, surrounded the police and dispersed the force. The crowd of the peasants captured two police officers. A police constable tried to save the lives of the officers and opened fire. Jhanku Singh was finally arrested. The crowd again attacked the police to save their leader but the police opened fire. Some peasants were killed and more than one hundred were wounded.[1]

On 23 March 1921, there occurred another bloody event. The prevention of "Seditious Meetings Act" was extended to the distrubed areas. The use of weepens was prohibited in four districts of Rae Bareilly, Pratapgarh, Faizabad and Sultanpur for a long period. The governmental authorities adopted repressive measures. The peasantry once again revolted. On the night of 17-18 April 1921, the Rae Bareilly collectorate was partially destroyed by them the police force began marches to frighted the peasants. The peasants organized the conferences on 11th May 1921 at Allahabad. The peasants of Awadh attended the meetings in large numbers. The non-cooperators tried to strengthen their hold on the kisan sabhas. On 13th May 1921 Pt. Jawaharlal Nehru arrived there. Afraid of his popularity, the government did not take any action against him. The peasant confrences and movements along with other activities of non-cooperation movement played a historical role in undermining the British power and prestige. The chief secretary to the Government of United Provinces reported to the home, department in Delhi on 13 May 1921, that the "situation is steadily deteriorating. The confidence in the power of government is growing less, officers are losing heart and the belief that the lives of Europeans are in danger, is growing.[2]"

On June 1921 the Viceroy telegraphed to the Secretary of state about the United Provinces that "There was little hope of peace in the areas of Agra and Awadh.[3]"

---

1. Sukhbeer Chaudhary ," Peasants and workers " Movement in India (1905-22) p. 92
2. Sukhbeer Chaudhary , " Peasants and workers " Movement in India (1905-22) p. 97
3. Ibid; p.97

5

The Gloom Deepens

In the region Awadh the Talukdari oppression had provoked the peasant revolts. Large groups of Kisans were changed in counter violence. They even attacked upon the Talukdari estates, destroyed their crops and property and looted the bazars, particularly the shops owned by merchants and money lenders. At some places they continuously used force to seem release of their arrested leaders and fellow kisans. The agrarian disturbances broke out in the form of desperate attempt to fight till the end. In those areas where Sabhas were very effective the peasants formed their own panchayats to set their disputes over. The agrarian agitation in Awadh had two distinguished features. At one level a section of tenantary was protecting the landlords and Zamindars. The peasants were strictly against evictions and nazranas. They mainly aimed at getting the occupancy rights for which they were trying to build pressures on the government to table a suitable legislative action. At the second level the peasants resistance took a more behavioural form in the sense that they only attacked the landlords and plundered markets. But soon these revolts turned into huge violence. The peasnats were not ready to suffer any more exploitation by the land lords who were in league with the alien rulers. The movement finally took the shape of an anti-imperialistic character.

The authorities tried to give some relief to the peasants against the landlords in order to satisfied them. The government enacted the "Rent Act for Awadh 1921". According to the new Act tenants received the right of owing the land for life. But the Act was not sufficient because most of the Awadh peasants were temporary tenants and subtenat and not the owners of land. They did not come under the category of permanent tenants and landlords continued to expel and evict them. Later the authorities themselves accepted that the Act was not quite sufficient. It only helped and improved the position of the rich and the high class peasants. The government which was trying to create a new foot hold in the villages failed in its objective. It tried to improve the condition of agriculture, but due to the deficiences of the act it could not do anything the discontent of the peasants grew deeper and inspired them to involved in the revolutionary activities.

In The United -Provinces After 1922

It was in 1922, when India was conducting whole heartedly the non-cooperation movement led by Mahatma Gandhi. Though being seperate non-cooperation movement and the peasant movement effected each other and a co-ordinatioin commonly existed between the two. Both of these movement caused by British exploitation. When the non-cooperation movement was on its extreme the entire country was trying hard to be free from British caused by British clutches yet in Chouri-Chaura in Gorakhpur district the police post was attacked by the patriots and the police opened fire on the revolutionary crowd. Many people died and thousands were injured. The angry crowd of the village burnt the thana and 21 police men died on the spot. After this incident, Mahatma Gandhi announced to stop the non-cooperation movement. Only one incident of violence by Indians upset him. This adjournment of non-cooperation movement disappointed the revolutionary peasants, and encouraged the British authorities. They became more oppressive and the target of their oppression and exploitation were mostly the poor peasants. This led to the rise of autonomous peasant organizations in the whole of India and also in the United Provinces.

The Aika Movement

The Aika (Unity) Movement challenged the oppressars, both the Talukdars and the British authorities. The "Awadh Rent Act" could not be successful in checking the peasant exploitation.

Since the Talukdars remained untouched by the act. The Congress leaders did not want to encourage any type of class struggle in the country. Gandhi wrote in 'Young India' that, "I hear the talk of even refusing payments of rent to Zamindars. It must not be forgotten that we are not non-cooperating with Zamindars. We must try to bring round the Zamindar to size, and isolated the big Zamindars. But if they will not come thus, we must be patient with them. We may not even proclaim a social boycott against them.[1]

M.N. Roy and Avoni Mukhorjee sent a manifesto to the Ahemdabad session of the Congress to get the peasants and workers behind. It was neeessry to widen the base of Congress. But nothing could be done because the Congress wanted the entire country to be united together.

The Aika or unity movement of Awadh, was organized by the peasants without the support of congress. According to M.N. Roy, "The Aika grew out of the Kisan Sabhas which had a very stormy history between 1920 and 1921 and whose revolutionary energy was lost by the non-cooperation propaganda for on undefined swaraj. A very acute out bursts at Rai Bareilly, Gorakhpur and Chauri-Chaura terrified the pacified leadership of the Congress. The betrayal of the national leaders and the activities of the officials inspired moderates to organize rival bodies called Aman Sabhas led to the burst of the movement again in the form of Aika Movement."[2]

The Aika Movement was started in Hardoi district of Awadh as early as 1921. After a silence during the summer season, further arised and became serious towards the end of 1921. Khwaja Ahmad was its leading spirit and its head quarter was situated at Malihabad in the Lucknow district.[3]

Baba Ram Chandra, the well known peasant leader of Awadh, had strong connection with the Muslim peasantry of Malihabad. After his convicton in March 1921, some 500 Pathan peasants

1. Mahatma Gandhi "Young India" 26/01/1922.
2. M.N.Roy International press Correspondence (Berlin), Vol-2, No. 51, 20/6/1922.
3. Police Abstract of Intelligence 4/3/1922, CID Records, Lucknow.

from Malihbad had decided to rescue him from the Lucknow jail. The name "Aika" expresed the unity of Hindu and Muslim peasants. The Aika union demanded privileges in favour of the large majority of the peasants. The land less poor labours and poor peasants were also involved in the movement. The programme of the union published in the Indian Daily News of 10 March 1922 contained six points:

1. The peasants will not leave the fields when illegally ejected;
2. Pay only the recorded rent;
3. Not pay rent without obtaining receipts;
4. Not do the BEGAAR of Zamindars;
5. Use the tank water for irrigation without any payment.
6. Graze their cattle in jungle without charges.[1]

Peasants took oath to follow these rules of Aika programme very strictly.[2] The revolutionary peasants adopted the policy of soical boycott towards those who refused to join the movement like washermen, barbers, sweepers who belonged to the lower classes. Socially boycotted the landlords and many of them abandoned the villages.[3] The whole of rural society included peasants united against the oppressors. They were united and gave a call to the people of Hardoi district, "Aika karo" (be United)[4].

In March 1922 the region of Awadh also faced a big explosion of the peasant's discontentment. By the end of February 1922 there held 21 Aika meetings in three days in the area of Hardoi district Large number of peasants from villages in the Malihabad. Tahsil of Lucknow, joined the Aika movement in Hardoi. At the time Madari Pasi was the chief leader of the AIKA party of peasants. He was a brave man-who was in his full command. He tried to strengthen the movement under his leadership. The government was looking for an opportunity to supress the Aika

1. MusKaliyov, The National Movement in India in 1921-22, Historical Journal Maskow 1940, p.85
2. Pioneer, 9/3/1922.
3. Kapil Kumar, "Peasant in Revolt" p.193
4. Indian Mirror, (Daily) 28 February 1922.

movement. The Zamindars favoured the Governmental decisions. The government used the cavalry to supress the movemnet and it was difficult to orgainze the movement in face of cruel repression and Madari Pasi had failed in his taks[1].

There occurred a clash between the police and the peasants in the village Udaipur in the Shahabad circile. Two peasants were killed in this struggle.[2] The situation at Kheri was described as "Unsatisfactory". In Kheri and Hardoi the peasants took part in the Civil Disobediences Movement led by Congress volunteers.

In Sitapur district the police burnt down the houses and huts of the poor villagers.[3] The administration used the terms of "badmash and "dacoity" to express the resistence of peasants, it was great injustice on the part of the government to suppress the movement with great cruelty. The authorities repress the Aika Movement because it did not have any strong base. Primarily it was a tenants' movement, thougth it was said that the Aika movement was more political in character. It was said because the non-cooperators and the Khilafatist zamindars helped it the beginning in Kheri and Hardoi.[4] In fact it was a low caste tenants' movement which grew up in the independent leadership of Madari Pasi and Sohrab. The restrictions of the organization only to lower level was also responsible for its short life, not more than four months.

The "No-Rent" campaign 1930-32

After the suppression of Aika Movement the peasants remained silent for a few years. The only organized movement at this time was the "No-rent" compaign of 1930, led by the Indian National Congress. Mahatma Gandhi had started the Civil Disobedience Movement in 1930 and it became necessary for the Congress to gain support of the Kisans for giving a form of a mass

1. Mazid Hayat Siddiqui, Agrarian Unrest in North India - The United Provinces p.202.
2. 'Leader' 16/3/1922
3. "Terrorism in the Sitapur district", in All India congress committee file NO. 5/1922.
4. Report on the internal political situation for January 1922, file No. 18/1922 Home Political Proceedings. The "No-Rent" compaiqh 1930-32

movement to the Civil Disobedience Movement, the conditions were favourable for them to exploit the long existing discontent due to the slump in prices that came with the depression of 1929-34.[1]

In the middle of 1928 Baba Ram Chandra a prominent leader of the peasant movement in Awadh orgainzed several meetings and inspired them to rise again.[2] Nehru visited Soviet Union in 1927-28 and became more radical to advocate agrarian problems after his return by his efforts the Kisan Sabha got a new starting in Basti, Gorakhpur and Faizabad regions. The Congress and Communists compainged in villages of Allahabad, Pratapgarh and Raebareilly district.[3]

Between October 1928 and June 1929 many political conferences were held all over U.P. The U.P. Congress Committee and the Communists both organized rallies in places like Lakhimpur Kheri, Jhansi, Rae Bareilly, Mainpuri etc. Pt. Nehru was the man who worked with full of his energy for the success of the new compaign. The abolition of landlordism, repudiation of tenants debts and other demands were raised at the national front the local grievances blended with national and political demands.[4] Later this collaboration of Congress and Communists helped Nehru to build up a "Left Wing" or "Socialist Lobby" within the Congress.

They also set "Youth Organization" in various universities and colleges and addressed many student gatherings. These efforts helped to make powerful the "No-Rent" campaign in Awadh, very powerful and significant .

In early 1930 the "No-rent" compaign started in Awadh. It was an important event with nation wide awakening. The Indian National Congress had launched the Civil Disobedience

1. D.N. Dhangare, Peasant Movenment in India 1920-50, P. 120.
2. Goverment of India- Home Department File No. 1-28 (political) January 1928.
3. Ibid; April-July 1928
4. (i) Government of India -Home Department File No. 17/29 (Political) February and June 1929.
   (ii) Report of the Delhi Provincial Political conference (13-15 October) President Pt. Nehru and held at Meerut.

Movement. It was partly related to the rural problems. The broken of salt laws was the main theme to the movement. The Salt Tax was the least oppressive of all the imperialist laws. But it was a symbolic protest and the rural population felt little involved in the Civil Disobedience because it was not even the least related to their more immediate agrarian problems. However the first phase of the civil disobedience movement failed to make any visible impact on the rural masses or the peasantry.

In October 1930, six months after the Civil Disobedience Movement had begun, there were no sings of "no-rent" campaign in the rural regions of U.P. It was Pt. Nehru, who after his release from the prison, started a no-tax" campaign.

Only towards the end of 1930, the Indian National Congress tried to gain the attention of the tenantry. Evictions increased as the landlords found it very difficult to collect the rent.

The government took two separate steps to contain the peasant discontent in U.P. The first was the Gandhi-lrwin meeting and a contract between the two known as Gandhi-lnrwin Pact. According to the Pact, the Civil Disobedience Movement including "non-payment of taxes, revenues and rent" was discontinued. As a result the no-rent" campaign of U.P. was called off before its full potentialities could be revealed. The Congress again worked against the will of masses.

Secondly, the government granted a remission of land revenue worth Rs. 17.5 million and brought pressure on their allies, the landlords, to make a similar gesture to their tenants by reducing rental rates proportionately.[1] It was an effort to earn the goodwill of the peasants.

The Congress leaders of U.P. stopped the "no-rent " compaign but only for a short time. Very soon, the government and the Congress began to find faults with each other and the Congress disputed the adequacy of the remissions in revenue and rents. The Congress also appointed a committee to enquire into the agrarian situation in the province of U.P. The Committee observed in its

1. Govenment of India-Home Department File No. 18A//31, Political May 1931

report that the peasnats of Awadh could get but only nominal relief. It reported that the remission in revenue was only 7 per cent while the total loss in the tenants assets on account of the fall in prices was nearly 60 percent.[1] The landlords share of deficit in next was only 8 percent.[2] So they did not lose as much as the peasants had lost.

In Awadh the peasant suffered on account of the system of illegal extortions and nazranas. Unlike their counterparts in Agra Provinces, the land-lords and land-owners in Awadh did not remit rents at the same rate as the government did allow the cut in the revenue. The tenantry in Awadh as a whole, therefore, got only a nominal relief vis-a-vis tenants in Agra Province.[3]

On the question of rents the important leaders of the Congress tried to compromise with the government. Gandhi met Sir Malcolm Hailey, the Governor of U.P. in May 1931 and issued a manifesto calling upon the tenants to pay their rents, to suffer but did not think of revange. The compromising attitude of Gandhi inspired Pt. Nehru and his left wing group in carrying forward the no-rent agitation. By the end of September 1931. Wellington replaced Irwin as Viceroy and Gandhi participated in the Second Round Table Conference held in London. Among such circumstances the U.P. Congress Committee decided to start the No Rent compaign again in Allahabad, Rae Bareilly, Unnao and Etawah districts.[4]

This renewed campaign in U.P. lasted effectively till the middle of 1931. Between December 1931 and July 1932 over 10,000 workers, volunteers and tenant agitators were cruelly convicted.[5] The British adopted the policy of suppression through out U.P.

The Congress started in full command the renewed agitation of 1931-32. The policy of non-violence parsued by the Indian

1. Agrarian Distress in the United-Provinces, U.P Congress Committee, Allahabad 1931, p. 12-13
2. Ibid:
3. Govt, of the U.P. Rent and Revenue Problems, Nainital 1934, pp. 5-6.
4. The Leader, November 18, 1931. P. 9
5. Government of India, Home Department File No. 18/05/32 (Pol.) March 1932.

National Congress led to very little violence by the peasants of Awadh. Both the peasnats and Congress agitators maintained a genuinely non-violent movement. Those who participated in the civil disobedience movement suffered represion quietly. The peasants also peacefully suffered all the tortures of the alien rulers. But their resistance continued. The disturbances in U.P. with regard to the "no-rent" agitation in 1930-32, can be analysed first in terms of their leadership and character and secondly in their effect in the distrubed areas. It can also be analysed in their relationship to Gandhian agrarion movements launched all over India.

It was earlier the local and religiously inspired leadership that moblised the poor peasants in Awadh districts. Urban elites had no appeal to the poor masses. In 1930-31, the "no-rent" agitation was a movement from above purely inspired by the nationalist leaders and the Indian National Congress. In 1930-32 the Congress was trying to establish its control over rural masses. The period of economic depression (1929-34) offered them a proper opportunity to prove their credentials. It used the peasant discontent for the growth of the nationalist movement. It was proved that the Congress could arouse the peasants for its own political ends.

Peasants' Struggle After 1935

Government of India till 1935 fully recognised the landlords and zamindars as true friends and became totally apathetic towards the peasants demands and agitation.

In 1935, the Government of India Act was regulated and in 1937 the provincial assembly elections were to be held. At this time in Uttar Pradesh the "Peasants and Workers Party" were strengthened. P. C. Joshi was the leader of the party and decided to launch a sepearate struggle for the peasants demands. The U.P. Congress Committee had a meeting on the 15th March 1936. Venkatesh Tiwari presented two resolutions and demanded in the meeting to organise a province wide peasant's sruggle. He insisted upon the members to prepare a minimum time bound programme for peasants under the guidance of the UP Congress Committee.[1]

1. The Leader (Allahabad) 18 March 1936

After the provincial elections of 1937, the Congress joined the government in U.P. Pt. Govind Ballabh Pant become the first Chief Minister of U.P. on 29 July 1937. Thousands of peasants marched to Lucknow and on 1 August, they organised a meeting in Aminuddola park of Lucknow. They presented a march under the banner of Congress and took oath for freedom. Pant admitted in Council that the Indian Nationl Congress was serious towards the peasants's demands in U.P.[1]

The Kisan Sabha

The Congress Socialist Party and some other individuals took a leading part in the formation of the Kisan Sabha. In its conference at Meerut, Jai Prakash Narain, the leader of the rally formed Congress Socialist Party and had a meeting with the peasant leaders of Madras and it was agreed upon to organise a representative conference of peasants at Meerut in January 1936. The Meerut conference decided to organise an All India Kisan Congress in April 1936 during the annual session of the Congress at Lucknow.[2]

As decided at Meerut, the "All India Kisan Congress" (which later changed its name as "All India Kisan Sabha") met at Lucknow on April 1936. Swami Sahajananda Saraswati, the leader of the Bihar peasants was the president of the Session. The Congress elected on All India Kisan Committee in which the Socialists, the Communists, and the Congress men were represented. The manifesto adopted at the Congress, declared that the object of the Kisan movement was to secure complete freedom from economic exploitation and the achievement of full econmic and political power for the peasatns, workers and other exploited classes, peasants to fight against their immediate political and economic grievances in order to prepare them for their emancipation from every form of political exploitation.

The fundamental demand of the Sabha centred on abolition of Zamindari and ownership of land by the tillers. The minimum

1. M.A.Rasul, A History of All India Kisan Sabha, p-22
2. N.G. Ranga, Kisan and Congress pp. 60-61

demands included moratorium of debts, abolition of land revenue and rent, licencing money-lenders, minimum wages for agricultural workers, fair price for sugarcane and commercial crops, irrigation facilities, gradual income tax, death duty and inheritance tax on the landlords and the merchants.[1]

Evidently the Kisan Sabha sought to reconcile the interest of all categories of peasants from the rich peasants to the landless labour and attempted to unite them of a common platform.

The preservation of peasant unity seemed to be the over riding consideration but the emphasis was on immediate demands which could be realised, so that it could appeal to the broad masses of peasants. The first of September was to be observed as Kisan Day to popularise the peasant demands, it was also decided to publish a weekly journal called "Kisan Bulletin" with Indu Lal Yagnik, the Gujrat Kisan Leader, as the editor of the Kisan Bulletion. It was to be published regularly to give a direction to the Kisan Movement in the formative phase, the formation of "All India Kisan Sabha" opened a new era in the history of the peasant movement. It branched out in provinces and united the peasant representatives from different parts of the country on a common platform.

In 1937, the meeting of the Kisan Council was held in Niyamatpur (Gaya, Bihar) in which K.M. Ashraf became the chief organiser. He organised a provincial peasant conference in Pilibhit in 1938. In the same year the U.P. Kisan Sabha joined it with the All India Kisan sabha and it was deemed as a branch of it. The represenatives of U.P. took part in Kummila (Bengal) conference of All India Kisan Sabha. At this time the number of All India Kisan Sabha Members form U.P. was about 60,000.[2]

The growth of peasant movements under All India Kisan Sabha exercised considerable pressure upon the Indian National Congress. In 1937 the Assembly election were to be held and so the Congress drew its attention towards peasant demands. In its Faizpur Congress session (December 1936) it paved the way

1. LP. Sinha , The Left Wing in India, 1919-47 pp-393-94.
2. M.A.Rasul, A History of All India Kisan Sabha, p-22

for the formation of an agrarian programme. Later it published a Congress manifesto in the elections of 1937. The Congress won its objectives through this manifesto and the allegiance of the peasants gradually shifted to the Congress. It gained the majority of votes in rural areas in the assembly election of 1937.

In the Kumilla Congress the peasant leaders had inspired the peasants to co-operate with the Congress in the struggle for complete freedom.[1]

The Kisan Sabha verified the aims of Kisan struggle and asserted that it was not ready for any compromises. The aim of the peasant movement was an agricultural revolution and they realised that the agricultural revolution was not possible without attaining Swaraj.

The U.P. Congress Committee decided to calebrate "Kisan Diwas" on 17th April in order to make the Kisan aware about land-tenure Act (Kashtkari Kanun).

In a governmental information, it was said that U.P. Kashtkari Kanun had been introduced in Assemblly which finally decided to send it to the select committee.

The Zamindar class showed strong reaction against the Kashtkari Kanun, but they were satisfied because the Kashtkari Kanun were not progressive enough to attack their vested interests.[2]

The elected government of U.P. fully supported the organisation of Kisan Sabhas at different cities and towns. The Indian National Congress was not ready to lose the support of landlords. But the U.P. Congress Committee refuse to compromise with landlords and it openly opposed the orders of the Congress.[3]

From among the 48 districts of U.P., 38 Kisan Sabhas were fully organised and powerful. In the middle of 1938 efforts were further made with All India Kisan Sabha for strenghening its

1. Report on Political Situation during forthnight ending 15 June 1939 Proceeding Home Department (Pol.)
2. Ibid.;
3. National Front Weakly, 7th August 1938.

position, it organised Press conferences, favoured up kashtkari kanun and demanded its enactment. On 26 October 1937 various conferences were organised rasied up the demands were reiteriated. Swami Sahajanand Saraswati, the leader of All India Kisan Sabha and a famous peasant leader of Bihar, made the tour of U.P. for two weeks. He addressed large peasant gatherings at Baneras, Gazipur, Balia, Bansdih etc. At every place large crowd celebrated his arrival and attended his lecture.[1]

On the month of October a conference of U.P. peasants was also held at Lucknow. Acharya Narendra Dev was on the chair. He expressed a hope that the zamindari system would be abolished. He appealed to the peasants to confine their struggle till they achieve the goal.

In November 1938 Swami Sahajanand Saraswati again started his tour of U.P. and addressed the peasant conferences in the districts of Fatehpur, Kanpur, Mirzapur, Moradabad, Mathura, Agra and other major places.[2] He appealed the gathering to strenghten the U.P. Kisan Sabha.

On 28 November 1938 the Agra district Kisan Congress was held at Fatepur Sikri. The peasants demanded the abolition of zamindari, without giving them any compensation.

The peasant conferences were also held at Ayodhya and Jhansi. The peasants were fully aware of their rights and they were ready for long struggle. They became able to resist any kind of oppression, whether by the zamindars as by the government.

The fourth conference of All India Kisan Sabha was held at Gaya in Bihar in April 1938 in which the demands of the peasants were again repeated.

From 1936 to 1939 was a period of organisation of the Kisan Movement. It made a rapid progress. After the Faizpur Conference, the peasant movement through Kisan Sabha successfully raised the peasants voice and the number of members increased from 5 lacs to 50 lacs. It had gained the form of a mass movement. The Kisan

1. Swami Sahajananad Saraswati, Mera Jeewan Sangharash, p. 53
2. Ibid;

Sabha organised its meetings at every place in the provinces. The peasant discussed the defective policies of the Government and expressed their feelings. There came the situation of violence and clashes between kisan and zamindars.

In a report of the Commissioner of Agra, there occurred a struggle between the peasants and the zamindars and a peasant was killed in the clash.[1]

In 1939 the popoular Government of U.P. had resigned on the question of the second world war in septermber 1939. The second world war was started and it created tensions in India. Many peasant leaders went underground due to the oppression to the government. After the August movement of 1942, violence broke out at many place in U.P. The government cruelly suppressed the movement in which the peasants suffered the most.

The Fifth Provincial Conferencne of Communist Kisan Sabha was held at Agra from 13 to 15 March 1943. After this Conference about ten Communist leaders were arrested at Bithur (Kanpur).

In 1944 the provincial conference of Kisan Sabha was held at Hathras. In this conference the govrnment was criticised on the issue of helping the sugar mill owners and suppressing peasants. Swami Sahajanand was the chief orgainser of this conference.[2]

After 1942, the U.P. peasants movement was mainly dominated by the Communist leaders, many Congress leaders left the Kisan Sabha. The Communist leaders organised it in a new way. Sajjad Zahir and Z.A. Ahmad made effective contribution to the peasants movement in the period. Dr. Z.A. Ahmad made tours of Unnao, Rae Bareilly, Pratapgarh, Ballia, Jhansi, Meerut, Sultanpur, Saharanpur, Aligarh etc. and tried to strengthen the Kisan Sabha.

The abolition of Zamindari was the main issue of the peasant struggles at this time. The U.P. Government also accepted the

1. Report on Political Situation during forthninght ending 15 August 1939, Proceeding Home Department (Pol.) File No. 18/8/1939
2. Report on Political Situation during forthninght ending 30 June 1944, File No. 18/8/1944.

principle of Zamindari abolition. The Zamindars became frustrated and started violence and oppression in the entire provinces. They cruelly killed the Peasants and their leaders. In June 1947 about 60 peasants and Kisan Sabha workers were killed and several of them were injured. The Zamindars organised their meeting at Lucknow. They said that they would save their zamindari through their swords.[1]

A landlord of Agra said that if Government took steps towards the abolition of Zamindari, there would be bloody violence all over. He also said that Zamindari should be adopted by the U.P. Government.

Abolition of Zamindari

The Congress adopted a dual policy on the question of the zamindari abolition. When it formed its Government it tried to organise the co-operatives. It permitted them legally to refuse their supply to the factories. The co-operatives were in a strong position in western and central districts of U.P. The Talukdars and Zamindars formed alliances of mutual benefit with the factory owners. They were in a large number in the best cane growing land of north. Thus controlling price and profits the zamindars profited from the co-operatives at the expense of their tenants, whose names were duly entered by the zamindars in the Society's register. It swelled the membership and thereby increasing the Governments allocation of seed, and fertiliser and credit to be given by the zamindars.

At the same time the Congress was also active in support of the anti zamindar peasant movement. On August 1946 on the eve of independence, the Congress resolved to abolish Zamindari legally. At the same time it also showed acceptance for paying compensation in return. The committee set up under the resolution to prepare a suitable scheme reported to the new Government in 1948 that the "Zamindari Abolition and Land Reforms" bill were presented to the legislative assembly."

The Zamindar class naturally opposed the Bill. They argued

1. People's Age, 13 October 1946.

that the Bill was not correctly designed. They said that the government in its ignorance would rather create mischief than remedy and it did not known even the basic facts about tenureship laws.

The government stood firm. It quite realised that no reform could be possible without the abolition of zamindari. G.B. Pant said while introducing the Bill, "in fact we have never been hostile to Zamindars or for that matter to any other section of the community. We wish to do all that we can for the welfare of every one, but all of us have to realise that the good of each individual lies in the good of all in this new order."

The method by which the Congress of U.P. proposed to reconcile the claims of the zamindars and the tenants, were by zero means and enelegant. A new system of tennure was to be established of four classes of tenants two major (Bhumidars and Sirdars) and two minor (Asamis and Adhivasis).

The Zamindars were to become Bhumidars in respect of their personal cultivation. The government was to acquire Zamindari rights in all property not covered under the head of personal cultivation and to pay the compensation for them. The tenants were to be redefined as Sirdars with permanent heritable (not saleable) rights in their holdings,"

The government's intention, consistent with its objectives and declared policy of decentralisation of the rural economy by reform then by revolution was not to extirpate the zamindars but rather to cut it down to size. The offenders of the Bill without any foresight argue that abolition might well prove beneficial to the majority of zamindars. Not surprisingly, the zamindars found it preposterous, an illdefined promise of solvency, for the zamindars who had managed without it for centuries it was no cosolation, so drastic a reduction in their property and their was palatabile of them they preformed to pit strength against the pasing of the bill and for the preservation of their estates in entirely, however unworkable. They organised meetings throughout U.P. After all as Nawabzada Hyder Ali had pointed out in the Sitapur Zamindars Conference in January 1947 that the zamindars were twenty lacks storng men and if only they organised themselves properly, no government would dare to ignore them, much less crush them. The battle against the passing of the reform aganist zamindari system was mainly fought in the legislative assembly on government ground. It was a foregone conclusion that the Bill would to be carried out. The Zamindari Abolition Bill finally became of the law in 1951. It was over a year, however, before its provisions could be brought into effect. The zamindars made a last legal offset. They inpugned the constitutional validity of zamindari abolition as contravening the fundamental right to property guarantee under Article 31.

The matter was settled by a decision of the Supreme Court and an important amendment was provided in the constitution, in favour of the state government in June1952. On 1st July 1952, the zamindari right were formally vested in the government.

The abolition of zamindari started a new era in Indian history. The free Indian brought independence for the peasants also for which they were waiting since decade. The zamindari system was the main cause of the peasants, expliotation but even now the poor in this country are suffering.

The zamindari class remained the rich class of society becasuse they captured industry, politics and administrative services. They somehow retained of India have been still divided in two classes of the big peasants and the land-labour the toiling millions for whom it still difficult to make the both ends meet.

6

◇◇◇◇◇◇

Relationship with Freedom Struggle

The fear of a peasants revolt in India had always haunted the British who were aware of the ineffective system of the steel frame which they had imposed upon this vast country.[1] The measures which they adopted in the late 19th century for the relief of debtors and the protection of tenants were all motivated by their political concern to strengthen their hold over the rural masses. They were not prompted by any reformative instincts. They succeeded in attaching the substance peasantry to enrich themselves.

It is striking to know that the peasant movement in U.P. possessed such a vast canvass that they always remained an integral part of the freedom sturggle directly or indirectly. The Great Reovlt of 1857 was the first explosion of anger and frustration of the Indians towards the evil policies of British. Later it become an example for the feedom fighters and the nationlists. Later this expression of anger and frustration become to be organized. The poverty of villages in India and specially in U.P. caused great dissatisfaction among the patriots. The exploitation and terror of landlords forced the peasants of U.P. to join the Indian National Movement. The national movement could not have been strong and complete wihthout the support ot its masses, specially the peasants and the tillers of the soil.

In rural India the anti-British or anti zamindari meant the same because both were working for exploitative purposes and were linked up with each other.

The British encouraged the landlords to pursue their interests and the landlords exploited government for support.

---

1. D. Rothermind, "Government, Landlord and Peasants in India", Agrarian Relations Under British Rule, 1865-1935.

The Indian National Movement would not have been without joining its masses to the main stream. The Indian National Movement in the early phase had its roots among the urban areas and it hardly touched the countryside.

When Gandhi emerged on the national stage for the first time expressed concern for the realities of the grass root level. He tried to carry the message of swaraj on the political freedom to the masses of India. He gave them a call for self reliance and national unity. On his call the inactive millions living in the rural India joined the movements conducted by the Indian national leaders. Other leaders of the Congress and the revolutionaries too remained isolated and unconnected with the villages. It was Gandhi's concept of non-cooperation and the civil disobedience that created a firm and true effect of the minds of Indian masses. After Gandhi assumed the leadership of the Indian National Congress, the peasant leaders came into his contact and broadened their base much more then just the landlord tenant conflicts. A feeling of attaining freedom form the clutches of the foreign government entered their minds. Gandhi knew well that the final challenge to British rule must come from the rural masses. For this he and the Indian National Congress needed a rural base. Gandhi was also aware of the fact that outbursts of the uncontrolled violence might weaken the movement and the British could easily crush them. As such Gandhi needed the peasants and the pesants needed Gandhi. He toured the villages and attracted the minds of the peasants.

The 20th century peasant movement of U.P. directly or indirectly influenced the Indian National Movement, the peasant movement took the first initiative in 1920-22 and it mainly emerged in Awadh region of U.P. Gandhi and Pt. Nehru met the peasant leaders and projected their demands under the banner of the Congress. They talked about the weaknesses of them quite freely. Both the leaders tell a burning need for collecting huge masses to join them. The lack of an adequate village network and that also of trained volunteers as well as the internal contradictions within the ranks of the National Congress caused them much anxiety. These were obvious impediments to a premature challenge of British rule. For these reasons, Gandhi was very cautions in his approach towards the nature of the national movement and about the velocity too.

In the beginning, the Indian National Congress did not interfere with the agrarian relations and did not raise those issues in its annual conferences. They remained unconcerned and unrelated to the economic grievances of the peasantry. It never wanted to start a movement for the class demands. It wanted to cover all sections of people and didnot want to lose the acceptance of the big and small alike and specially of zamindars and the landlords Pt. Nehru wrote, "Non-cooperation and peasant movement were separate issues although both inspired each other in U.P. The Swarajaya was a vast term in which all these things were included collectively.[1]

If the agrarian disturbances of 1921-22 were somehow inspird by non-cooperation and Khilafat movement, it was indeed just coincidental. But in the case of "no-rent" campaign, it was fully inspired and effected by the national policies and the Civil Disobedience Movement sponsered by Gandhi. The agrarian unrest burst forth at a time which provided a great chance to draw the peasantry into the feedom struggle. The national leaders said that the Congress would lose its credibility if it remained aloof from the peasant movement. Pt. Jawaharlal Nehru emerged as the chief spokesman of peasantry and the U.P. Congress Committtee took up the initiative and lead in expousing the peasant cause.

By October 1930 the agrarian unrest in the western parts of the United Provinces had reached a point where it urgently required an organisation and an articulation. Without it, the outbrust would be limited to a series of local clashes. The conference committee provided the network for them and the peasants found a suitable leadership in the Congress leadership. Most of the leaders of U.P. Congress Committee came directly from the ranks of the peasantry. The closing of the peasant movement with the national movement designed by the urban elites was rather a complex

1. Pt. Jawarhalal Nehru, An Autobiography, p. 59

process which has been described in a recent study as a case of limited moblisation.[1]

If one considers the communication gap between the peasantry and the urban leadership the kind of approchment which was established between the two, remained fairly impressive. A few of urban leaders had the detailed knowledge of agrarian affairs and of the economic situation of the peasntry.

Their eagerness to learn more about the exploitative forces and to establish contacts with the masses of the countryside was greatly to their credit.

The peasantry on the other hand showed courage and endurance in their own struggle as well as in the intimated movement. It could be easily intimiated by a show of force and the traditional methods of rural oppression in which the police and the guards of the landlords were post masters. But indirectly they organized the masses of the peasantry as a storng force to combat them as well as the foreign rulers.

As Sitla Sahai a Congress man from Rae Bareilly put it in a letter to Pt. Jawahar Lal Nehru, "It seems to me that the Kisan Changes suddenly from one mood to another. The presence of a Congress worker inspires him and his absence depresses him. This means that we have to spend a lot of our time living with him before he can be expected to take a bold step at his own initative. And there were not enough Congress workers who could live with the peasants so as to learn from them and to encourage them in their quest for emanicipation. At the height of the "No-Rent" campaign of 1930, most of the Congress leaders were any how imprisoned the work had to be left to the new recruits . It is amazing that many of them did very well, indeed but nevertheless could not hope to cover the vast rural areas of the United Provinces. But the message that the Congress was with the peasants spread everywhere and this was an important factor for the future political development in this region."

---

1. Gyanendra Pandy, The Ascendancy of the Congress in Uttar Pradesh, 1926-34, A Study in Imperfect Mobilization, Delhi 1978

The Gandhi-lrwin pact of 1931 was a severe setback to this new solidarity. The economic condition of the peasantry had become professionlly worse in the winter of 1930-31 when the wheat prices had reached its lowest point and the government ot the united provinces had not yet implemented any measures of relief. At this time a report written by Pt. Nehru on the subject of U.P. Provincial Congress Committee and the economic distress in the rural areas was handed over to the Government of India by Gandhi.[1] The debate about the reasons which compelled Gandhi to conclude this pact has not yet come to an end. The message received from the business community, which was hit by the severe financial strigency prevailed at that time and could no longer provide the funds for we required the maintenance for the Congress organisation may have been of some importance in this respect.

Lord Irwin's skilful diplomacy was certainly another decisive factor. Irwin wanted to break the alliance between the Congress and the peasants and he was eager to get Gandhi involved in the process of the constitutional reforms by securing his attendance in the Second Round Table Conference. Gandhi did not want to betray the cause of the peasants nor was he interested in the constitutional reform which the British designed for India, but he accepted Irwin's offer which interpreted as a change of heart because it provided him an opportunity to complete his symbolic revolution with the important symbolic act of meeting the viceroy on equal terms, a fact which Churchill summed up very well in his notorious reference to Irwins encounter with the "half-naked faqir of India".

While concluding this pact Gandhi submitted a detailed memorandum concerning the plight of the peasantry to the Government of India. But this did not help the peasants who were soon made to feel what this pact held for them. The landlords and their Lenchmen pounced upon the peasants telling them that now they had to pay up because there was a truce between the

1. Congress Report for the year 1930 Prepared by Nehru, FICC file G- 2, 1931.

Congress and the government. Gandhi tried to mediate between the government, the landlord and the peasants. But his initiatives were answered with the assurance of the Governor of the United Provinces that it was his government's policy to hold the scales even between the landlord and the tenant. This was, in fact what Gandhi also wanted to do and the government did not want to give him a chance to assume this central role which was so essential for the maintenance of the British rule in the rural side. The summer of 1931 was the time of a constant tog of war between the Congress and the government of the United Provinces and Jawahar Lal Nehru probably did not exaggerate when he wrote to G.B. Pant that, "the government is trying to break U.P. and the agrarian situation? The government adopted the policy to defeat the Congress movement in countryside and did everything for this. The Governor said that in this way the Congress was spoiling for peasants another fight and increasing the peasants militancy in Allahabad district. This created an open conflict. This district was obviously affected by the decline of the rice price in the beginning of 1931. The harvests had not been good, and the occupancy tenants accounted for 80 percent of tenantry in this district were deprived by their landlords of their occupying right as arrears of rent could not be paid. The movement grew up and Allahabad had not been inthe vanguard of the "No-Rent" campaign of the previous year, but it now emerge as the "Bardoli of the United Provinces."[1]

The new "No-Rent" campaign in Allahabad and in several other districts of the united provinces began even before the return of Gandhi from the Second Round Table Conference. But at this time the whole Congress leadership was imprisoned and the government practically declared a total war against the Congress. The peasants movement was defeated by a policy of remission and repression and in May 1932 the government of United Provinces issued a press circular in which it stated that the campaign could definitely be said to have failed.

The British had undoubtedly won this battle but in the long

1. Gyanendra Pandy, The Ascendancy of the Congess in Uttar Pradesh, 1926-34, A Study in Imperfect Mobilization, Delhi 1978

run they lost the war. The allegiance of the peasants gradually shifted to the Congress. This became obvious in the elections which were held in 1936. When and extended franchise included the sbustantial peasants voted for the Congress. This support of masses strengthened the nationality of Congress and gave energy to the movement; definitely the peasant movemnet of U.P. had become a part of the national movement. At the same time it had its own thinking, concepts and principles. The peasant movement in many ways appears to be inspired by the Russian Revolution and Marxism. The leaders of Indian peasant movement were affected by the thoughts and philosophy of the Russian Revolution.

The Communists became the pioneers of socialist thinking in Indian freedom movement. They were related with the left wing of the Congress and the Socialist and Communist parties. The organizations of Kisan Sabhas were dominated by the left wing or the socialist group of the Congress.

The peasant movements of U.P. thus in 20th century assumed a nation wide political shpae and submerged with the non-cooperation and civil disobedience movements.

The Indian freedom movement caught fresh wind from its soil when peasantry of this country joined it. Heroic fights occurred in Rae Bariellly, Sultanpur, Faizabad and in the whole region of Awadh. During the struggle it was inspired by different socialist thoughts and philosophy. After the suspension of the non-cooperation movement by Gandhi, it was influenced by the Socialists who challenged the Gandhian theory of non-violence, "Is it the way to wipe out tears from every eye?" the sudden suspension of non-cooperation movement inspired the masses to join a long but active and uncompromising struggle against the British the "No-rent" campaign of U.P. launched in 1930-32 was dominated by the "left-wingers" of Congress , who were not ready ot accept Gandhi's policy of peace, compromise and collaboration, Nehru and his socialist lobby played an important part in the entire process and successfully aroused peasants to attain their political goals, the managed to present them before the British government as the most discontented part of Indians and handled a powerful issue to criticize the alien rulers. After 1935 the peasants received their directions from the Kisan Sabha which was dominated by the "left-wing" of the Congress. The Congress was a multi-class organisation and it did not want to lose the support of the zamindars or the landlords. So responsibility to continue the peasant struggle fell upon the Communists, the Socialists and the Congress men of socialist temperament. They all worked thorugh the Kisan Sabhas in U.P. The peasant organizations were established in1934 under the presidentship of P.D. Tondon. In April 1936, U.P. Peasant Organisation became a branch of AIKS and widened its base.

After 1938 Congress adopted the theory that the uprising of peasant orgainzation would give birth to class struggle and it will not be beneficial for the Indian National Congress. The Congress viewed it as a panelled organisation

Though the fear of Congress was without any logic and it proves its narrow and self countered outlook. Indulal Yagnik wrote in Kisan Bulletin that the peasant organisations or Kisan Sabhas were not the parellel organizations of Congress. In fact they were also strugglling against the exploitation of the peasants by the British government and working for the strength of the Indian National Congress. In fact the Congress ultimately realised the fact.

The period from 1936 to 1947 was the best part of the national movement. It had become a mass movement and spread like wildfire in villages. The dissatisfaction and exploitation of the peasants fully came in to the lime light and they became fully awakened and alert for their rights and duties both. The demand of zamindari abolition was raised with full strength and finally they won the battle when Congress come to power in free India.

In short, there was a candid co-relationship and sure connection between the freedom struggle and the peasant movements of U.P. Had it not been that both of the movements would not have succeeded in such a grand style. Both of these were not complete and realistic without each other. They were complementary and supplementary to each other. The peasant movement provided the grass root approach to the Indian freedom struggle and it was indeed Its greatest contribution in the national movement of India.

7

Personalities

Among the nationalists a few dynamic leaders took up the cause of peasant classes and emerged as very powerful and significant leaders of the period. Indra Narain Dwivedi was one such leader who started a U.P. Kisan Sabha at Allahabad with Home Rule League funds in February1918. He had in mind a fairly electoral purpose. It was the time when the massive world war had come to an end and its social and economic consequences were keenly felt in India. It sharpened the numerous contradictions between the Indian interests and British exploitations, like the drain of wealth, the decline of handicrafts, revenue pressures and obstacles to indigeneous capital growth. According to Dr. Sumit Sarkar, "The war affected the Indian life through massive recruitements, heavy taxes, war loans and a ver;y sharp rises, in prices, and it may be directly related to the two fold extension of the national movements - towards considerable sections of the peasantry and towards business groups."[1]

Indra Narain Dwivedi was a person quite patriotic and he was full of nationalist ideals. He brought the peasants very near to Indian National Congress. He stood for the principle of massive peasant's supprot to the Congress movement against the British imperialism. He also attempted to attract the peasants towards the ideals of Hinduism. He supported the move of cow protection and the propaganda undertaken by the Sanatana Dharma Sabha of Allahabad in this regard. Indra Narain Dwivedi was himself a Sanatan Dharma activist of Allahabad. He combined, in his lectures to the peasants the religious preachings with the atticacy of Home Rule politics. He also advocated the use of Hindi in personal and official work.

1. Sumit Sarkar : Modern India p 269;

Baba Ramchandra was not only an eminent peasant leader of Rae Bareilly but he was also very popular among the rural people. His organization was initially quite autonomus and was related to the problems of the grass roots peasants. It was Baba Ram Chandra who concentrated upon the grass roots peasants. It was Baba Ram Chandra who concentrated upon the genuine problems of the peasants of U.P. It was his efforts that Bedakhali was stopped in the regions of Pratapgarh. He ably led considereable section of the peasants of Awadh. The British had done their best to win over the Awadh Talukadars. They remembered their very strong resistance in 1857. They wanted to give a free hand to them regarding the tenancy with a view to get more revenue for themselves. Baba Ram Chandra was a sanyasi who come to Rae Bareilly as an indentured labour from Fizi. He was totally devoted to the Kisan Sabha and the solidarity of the Kisans. He often recited Ramayana for the peasants and raised caste slogans to unite them in close bonds of brotherhood and unity. He started his office at Roor village in Pratapgarh. He also united the lower castes and founded the Kurmi Kshatriya Sabha. His demands were fairly moderate as reduction of cesses and abolition of Begaar, refusal to cultivate Bedakhli, social boycott of oppressive landlords througth the Panchayats. The British government arrested him on a trumped up theft charge and the peasants of Pratapgarh demonstrated in a massive crowd to get him released.[1]

The real name of Baba Ram Chandra was Shridhar Balwant Jodhpurkar. He was born in 1864 in a Gwalior village. He left his home due to family funds and worked as a labourer in the city. In 1908 he went to Fizi as an indentured labourer. As he was Maharashtrian brahmin and the job as a labourer was below his dignity he change his name as Ram Chandra. He learnt the lesson of freedom as a labourer in Fizi where he stayed till 1916. He took an active part in the movement for the freedom of indentured labourer. He was considered to be a successful agitator in Fizi. For fear of punishmet, he fled away from there and settled at Azamgarh in U.P. He became safe from the arrest by the Fizi Government.

1. Home politcal (Confidential) FNo. 75 February 1920

He widely travelled the province of U.P. He delivered lectures against the evil practice of indentured labour. In 1919 he finally settled in the Pratapgarh district. He was constantly under the vigil of the police and was held responsible for spreading disaffection among the peasantry. He incited the peasants against the practice of Nazrana and Bedakhli. Jawaharlal Nehru wrote about him that, "Ram Chandra came as a saviour of peasants and he had tremendous powers of organizations."[1]

Ram Chandra's objective in organizing the peasant's movement was to make it caste-based. He contacted the leaders of the Panchayats of various castes and mobilized and peasatns through them, he worked very sincerly and dedicatedly and was able to secure the confidence of the people. Ram Chandra acknowledge that at Pratapgrah, as many as twenty time the Kisan Sabhas worked under the guidance of Jhinguri Singh and Durgpal singh.[2] He occasionally visited Sultanpur and other near by villages and recited the Ramayana every where, he was able to learn the dialects of the eastern U.P. and his recitals were very much appreciated every where. The zamindars of Azamgarh organized 'Bhandaras' for him[3]. When he visited their house on the occasion of 'Guru Purnima'.

The innocent masses of the villages began to recognize him as a holy person full of spiritual power. Baba Ram Chandra encouraged mass dining in the Bhandaras. It was a new concept of unity in the eastern villages of Awadh. Baba Ram Chandra was a venerated peasant leader of the eastern U.P. He often published pamphlets illustrating the exploitation of the Zamindars and highlighting their high handed behaviour towards the oppressed and the poor. He instilled a new hope among the fear stricken frustrated peasants[4].

Ram Chandra in the begininig of the peasant movement under proprietors of thirty-six villages in the districts of Jaunpur and

1. J.L.Nehru - An Autobiography London 1936 p. 51.
2. Mehta's Report p.7
3. Ibid; pp. 657.
4. Jawaharlal Nehru op cip p. 55

Sultanpur who had formed a union for their own econmic and moral gains. He pleaded the need of amity and goodwil among the rural people and specially the agricultural masses.[1] Later he wrote another pamphlet exhorting the peasants to pursue a well defined programme which geared then towards self-help and combined efforts. It were his teachings that led the peasants to break their age-long silence and be actively engaged in their agitation.

In June 1920 Baba Ram Chandra led a few hundred tenants to Allahabad from the Janupur and Pratapgarh districts. He met there with Jawaharlal Nehru and Pandit Gauri Shankar Misra. Since then Jawaharlal Nehru became an ordent champion of the peasants interests. Ram Chandra and thirty two other peasatns were charged of theft by the police. As a reaction some five thousand peasant assembled in a violent mood and demanded his release from the jail.[2] After ten days, they assembled again and held a violent demonstration. The authourties smuggled him out to the jail and secretly released him in the military camping ground. From the top of a tree, Baba Chandra had a glimpse of the sixty thousand peasants and villagers who were standing in the field. It was a symbolic and foreceful triumph of the Kisans. He remained active in the peasants movements throughout his life.

The most famous booklet ot Baba Ram Chandra was *Ab Bhi Ankhe Kholo Kisan.* He devised indigenous methods for the propagatioin of his programme, he was one who provided the peasants with an opportunity to know each other closely and discuss common problems. He invested a new meaning to the old slogan of Sita Ram's religious story. He also attempted to enlist the cooperation of the district authorities to accoopmlish his misson. He wished to expand the horizon of the movement by bringing Mahatma Gandhi and other educated urban leaders into it. He frequently visited Allahabad for this purpose and came in contact with P.D. Toandon, Jawaharlal Nahru and Pandit Gauri Shankar Misra, K.K. Malviya and many others. Jawahar Lal Nehru was

1. Pamphlet issued to the peasants by Baba Ram Chandra.
2. Times of India Dated 24 oct. 1920.

stunned to see the organizing capacity of the peasants under his leadership.

Baba Ram Chandra intersified the struggle by asking the peasants to with held the illegal exactions and stop cultivating the Sirlands of the cruel talukadars.[1] He also introduced the boycott principle for those who did not cooperate with the peasants' mainstream. He was considered to be a Bolshevik again by the Chief Secretary of U.P.[2] He was in fact the godfather for the peasantry. He link up the energies of the peasants with the ultimate goal of swaraj.

The peasant leaders like Baba Ram Chandra used to reach the Hindu-Muslim unity and brotherhood of the rural people. Their slogan was the unity of cultivators. They also encouraged the use of swadeshi and education for children. Baba Ram Chandra desired the extension of railway and roads to rural regions, he paid frequent visits to several villages and organized several units of the Kisan Sabha. He galvanized the silent rather the mute masses of peasantry to action. He toured on foot and observed the Kisan day on 20th December 1921.

Jhinguri Singh and Sahdev Singh were also the leaders who joined Baba Ram Chandra and worked with him. They were disgruntled under proprietors of Partapgarh. Jhunguri Singh was a fire brand person and was very active in the peasants movement of U.P. another radical leader of the peasants of Hordoi, Bahraich Bara Banki and Sitapur districts was Madari Pasi. He demanded the conversion of produce rents into cash. He inspired the peasants to take collective oath to fight till the last. The elaborate rituals were performed and the mantras were recited collectively under his guidance. Madari Pasi was ultimately arrested by the British police in June 1922. Though he belonged to a low caste and possessed some control over lower casted masses in the rural regions, he did not enjoy the full supremacy and unrivalled position. Many people

1. The land revenue per head of population in Awadh was almost four times then in the permanently setteled Bengal.
2. Letter of Chief Secretary File No. 358/1920.

of his own caste did not like his rise and became his enemies. Yet he was dedicated to improve the condition of poor peasants.

Krishan Dutt Paliwal was an eminent political leader of Agra district. He was a staunch Congressman and he led the peasants to conduct a non violent agitation against the British. He favoured the non-payment of taxes , mass desertion of villages in face of cruel police action. He did not allow them to indulge in violence against the landlords or even the British officers, he was also the follower of Gandhiji. He was the chief editor of the newspaper 'Sainik'. This newspaper ventilated the grievances of the poor peasants.

Another eminent personality was Kalka Prasad who guided the peasants to withhold the rent. Though the pressure was high upon him for redical action, he controlled the peasants and diverted them to peaceful resistance. Gandhiji always used to check the agrarian radicalism but whenever they found an opportunity they did not hesitate in indulging in violence. Kalka Prasad was driven out of the District Congress Committee. The result of his exit gradually quitened the movement. The peasant movement of Rae Bareilly also overpowered by the Congress programme as announced by the central organization under the leadership of Gandhiji.

Seth Achal Singh was another prominent leader of the peasants' movement. He was firstly a staunch follower of Gandhiji. This was the reason why Agra peasant movement was comparatively peaceful and slow. He invited Gandhiji to visit Agra and informed him of the possibilities of attracting the peasants to the non-violent movement of the Indian National Congress. He made the peasants of Agra to realize the efficiency of No-Tax campaign. He frequently went to meet the peasants and the often extended financial help to them. He was very philanthropic and generous.

Deo Narain Pande and Kedar Nath were the two peasant leaders of Sultanpur and Faizabad respectively. They organised the peasants in their regions. Baba Janki Das and Baba Badri Narain Singh was another leader of the peasant movement, many of these leaders were influenced by Baba Ram Chandra and Mahatma

Gandhi. Kashi Prasad was an influential peasant leader. Pandit Ramlal Sharma was very active leader of the village Prayagpur in the district to Sultanpur. Thankurdin was a staunch peasant leader of Kotia and Mahauli in Pratapgarh. Thakurdin's activites surprised Baba Ram Chadra who gave him the name of lion. He was convicted for four years imprisonment. At Rae Bareielly Matabadal and Amol Sharma and at Faizabad Lallanji and Kedar Nath were also very committed peasant leaders who organized the Yudha March of the peasants in 1920. Kalka Prasad toured the villages of Rae Bareilly district and delivered fiery speeches to incited the peasants for violent action. Salik and Ram Awtar were called the ring leaders of the peasant movement in U.P. because they too incited violence against the cruel zamindars. Both of them were ultimately arrested by the police. Suraj Prasad and other leader was also arrested with seventeen other peasants and all of them were sent to Faizabad jail.[1]

Along with Kedar Nath and Deo Narain, Raghunandan Sadhu was another prominent peasant leaders who organized Kisan Sabha movement in Sultanpur. Their activities and speeches banned the simmering discontent of the peasantry into and open revolt. Brijpal Singh of the village Marhwan in the district of Pratapgarh attributed the distress of the tenants to the high handedness of the estates manager and demanded his termination from the service. His friends supported him in this cause. Surajpal Singh Gangadin and Jhunku Singh also demanded the dismissal of the manager. They organized a large demonastration to prove their strength but the police opened fire on the crowd and they all dispersed.

Pandit Motilal Nehru remained the President of the U.P. Kisan Sabha for many years. He issued to the Kisans a leaflet entitled, "*Kisano ko Sandesh*," emphasizing upon the need of hard labour and sacrifice on the part of the peasants to attain swaraj. He insisted that the movement should remain quite non-violent and the peasants should follow the non-cooperation programme of the Congress. Janki Das was another peasant leader of eminences

1. Leader, Dated 25/11/1920

Pandit Martand Vaidya was the Vice-President of the District Kisan Sabha. He was arrested on the complaint of a talukadar named Amar Pal Singh for destroying the furniture of his house and the vegetables in his fields.[1]

Pandit Jawaharlal Nehru was a very popular Congress leader who worked among the peasants. He extensively toured the entire rural regions of U.P. and be friended the peasants. He attempted to remove their grievances and tried to solve their internal quarrels. he initiated unity among the peasants.

Madari Pasi and Soharab were the members of Eka Sangh who organized the lower caste peasantry. But they were badly crushed by the imperialistic government. Who treated them as dacoits and anti-social elements.

P.D. Tandon and Ram Nath Tripathi were also prominent leaders of the peasants' movement. Pandit Gobind Ballabh Pant was elected as the Vice President of the U.P. Kisan Sabha. Baba Ram Gulam another leader was a friend of Baba Janki Das. He was imprisoned for inciting the peasants tortured in the jail. A Kisan Seva Sangh was established in Makrahi village of the district Balia. Bachu Ram Singh Yadav and Ram Lagan Gupta belonged to this organization. Bachu Ram attracted the attention of the people towards the sad plight ot the peasants in Faizabad district and pin pointedly wrote in the newspaper 'Pratap' regarding the exploitation (*Bedakhli*) of peasants. Ram Lagan Gupta wrote an article in the same paper complaining of the cruelties of the zamindars towards the peasant leader of the Bihar province but this influence was disernible over the peasants of U.P. P.C. Joshi organized a party and named it as "Workers' and Peasants' Party". In western U.P. Swami Sahajanand, Mohanlal Gautam and Maharshi Purushottam Das Tandon decided to establish an all India organization to reflect the grievances of the vast majority of Indain peasants. Later in 1935 the Congress Socialist Party appointed two persons. Prof. N.G. Ranga and Jai Prakash Narain as Conveners to convene an All India Kisan Conference. The important leaders of this organizations were besides Swami

1. Abhuduya (Weekly) 8/8/1937.

Sahajanand Saraswati and N.G. Ranga, Indulal Yagnik, Mohanlal Gautam, K. M. Ashraf, Sohan Singh Joshi, Ahmed Kamal Sarkar, Sudhir Pramanik, Jai Prakash Narain and Ram Manohar Lohia. All of them were unanimous in recommeding that zamindari must be abolished. Indulal Yagnik was assigned the responsibility of editing a fortnightly bulletin in 1936. The same year with the efforts of P.D. Tandon, the U.P. Kisan Sangh was established. K.M. Ashraf was appointed the convener for its first conference. Raja Maheshwari Dayal and Shaikh Jabibullah were among those who backed the demands of the peasants by their speeches and writings.

In the meeting of peasants of Jaunpur district Sampurnananda, Shri Prakasha and Lal Bahadur Shastri gave expression to their sentiments in favour of the peasants of U.P. Pandit Govind Ballabh Pant who presided over another meeting at Sultanpur warned the peasants of adopting the violent methods. All these were prominent men of the Congress party and they found an opportunity to make the Congress a political forum with a mass appeal. The peasants represented the poor masses of India. The British government too realized it. The peasant leaders were attracted towards the action of the congress and they found an opportunity to join the main stream of the national movement. But it was in a way lip sympathy that the Congress leaders possessed for the peasants. No Congress leader was of the statue of Baba Ram Chandra who lived and died for the common cause and the peasants.

Baba Raghav Das was an eminent peasant leader of eastern U.P. He pointed out towards the sad plight of the peasants in Gorakhpur and Deoria districts. The governmnt faced lot of difficulties in realizing the taxes from the peasants of these districts. The peasants of Gorakhpur region under his able leadership refused to pay any kind of tax and resisted with all might the government karkuns.[1] The Revenue Minister of U.P. had to survey the Gorakhpur region for assessing the correct position. It was on the insistence of Baba Raghav Das that the peasants of this region insissted for a receipt from the Govt.

1. U.P.Govt. File Dated 18/7/1937.

Dr. Ashraf Ali, though he belonged to Gaya, Bihar, was appointed Convener of the Kisan Sabha of U.P. and he organized a conference at Peelibheet. He encourged the peasants of U.P. to participate in the All India Conferece of the Kisan Sabha, the central body.

Swami Sahajanand Saraswati also belonged to Bihar. But as he was the General Secretary of the All India Kisan Sabha, he visited the rural areas of Awadh region. He advised the peasants to observe their "Demand Day" and hold demonstration at different places.[1] After his tour of U.P., he published a critical report and revealed the cruelties of the British authorities. He again appealed for the need of accelerating the peasant movement in U.P.

Vishambher Dayal Tripathi was a socialist. He organized a meeting of the peasants at Unnao. Acharya Narendra Dev was in the chair. Both of them supported the directions of Kisan Sabha in this regard Arjun Arora was the leader of the labourers and workers of Kanpur. Under his guidance, more than 50 thousand workers expressed their allegiance with the struggle of the peasants.

When the All India Kisan Sabha was convened at Lucknow, Prof. N.G. Ranga, B.P. Dwivedi, Indulal Yagnik, Bankim Mukerjee, Awadhesh Prasad Sinha and Miyan Iftekharuddin addressed the peasants. They were also elected the office bearers of All India Kisan Sabha.

Mohanlal Gautam was a prominent Congress leader but he was elected as the Secretary of the U.P. Kisan Sangh. He made hectic efforts to solve the problems of the peasants of U.P. He participated in the demonstrations of the peasants in the district of Allahabad and talked to Jawaharlal Nehru about the nature and extent of the peasants problem.

Bhisma Arya was the Secretary of the District Kisan Sabha of Allahabad. He encouraged the peasants to pressurize the authorities for checking the armed attacks of Zamindars. Lal Bahadur Shastri and Saligram Jayaswal also helped him in organizing the peasants and inciting them to protest boldly against all injustice and crime.

1. U.P Govt. File Dated 18/7/1937.

Kunwar Nihal Singh was an eminent peasant leader of Hardoi. He was quite young and energetic. In a village named Gobardhan of Hardoi district the servants of the cruel zamindars, who had snatched away vast tracts of land from the peasants, attacked upon Kunwar Nihal Singn. He was blamed and held responsible for the protest of the peasants. He was finally killed six other peasants who were his trusted followers were also killed with him.

Jata Shankar Shukla was a leader of the peasants of Unnao. Ramesh Sinha was a leftist but he also supported the peasants movments of U.P. through his speeches and writings.

In the Fatehpur circle of Azamgarh district, the Zamindar's men attacked the house of a peasant leader, Rameshwar Prasad. His family members were badly hurt in the encounter. In the Banaras district, Hamiduzatar, Gopal Paranjape and S.P. Tripathi were very popular peasant leaders. The government tortured these leaders and levied upon them, the article forty four. They were inspired and enthused by the tours of Swami Sahajanand who visited Benaras, Ghazipur, Balia, Sahatwar and Bansideeh. He was honoured and huge gatherings of peasants attended his meetings. He also visited Fatehpur, Agra, Mathura, Kanpur, Shanjahanpur, Etawah, Moradabad and Mirzapur. His visits proved great encouragement to the peasant masses.

Acharya Narendra Dev too became very active in peasant politics. He was the Chairman of U. P. Kisan Sangh and the U.P Kisan Conferecne. Acharya Narendra Deo organized a peasant's conference at Ayodhya and narrated in detail the history of U.P. Kisan Sabha since 1921. Many demands were placed before the government in favour of the peasants in this Conference.

Vijay Singh Pathik was a popular peasant leader of Fatehpur Sikri. He demanded the abolition of zamindari without payment of any compensation. In 1935, Ajit Prasad Jain who was the Revenue Minister addressed a huge peasants gathering. Arjun Arora was a popular peasants leader of Kanpur. It was he who increased the membership of the Kisan Sabha and did commendable services to this movement.

The list of the peasant leaders in various parts of U.P. brings to our notice many glaring facts of history. It was not always necessary for the peasant leaders to be educated and trained. Their rise was quite abrupt and once they jumped in the battle for their tenancy rights. They themselves were not aware of the results. They were not concerned at all with the Congress movement of the period. Their own bread and butter initiated them to rebel against the zamindars and the imprialist administrations. But many of the leaders were the Congressmen who wanted to strenghten their movement with the presence of the peasants there. Some of the peasant leaders attanded the annual conferences of the Indian National Congress and joined the membership of the U.P. Congress committee. The interaction of the peasants with these organizations yielded good results. The peasants became aware of the British imperialistic designs and they cultivated a national outlook.

The peasant movemets of U.P. generally remained quite peaceful. The initial outbreaks and violence ultimately stopped. Violence did not become an objective of the peasant movement. Besides, the cruel treatment of the British administrators who crushed them was very harsh. They were either punished or their moral tone was destroyed. The leaders of U.P. Congress Committee did not take up their cases in the law courts and they were helpless before the criminal proceedings against them. Later they also became peaceful and the peasant leaders preferred for them to follow the passive resistance. The Congress ultimately came to realise their callous behaviour towards the arrested peasant leaders and changed its attitude towards them.

The peasant leaders wrote a marvellous chapter in the history of peasnat's movement for they did not fear the force of the government. They were not properly trained for a revolution. They were perfect patriots and real representative of the Indian masses.

They could gather in large number within no time. They were treated cruelly by the zamindars. The British authorities too maltreated them. They were victims of double torture and punishment. The peasant did not rise suddenly their leaders emerged from their tortured groups in the begning. But many of the leaders stood up with them when they really realized their sad plight. The leaders of the peasants movement possessed a broad horizon of thought and a deep sympathy with the masses.

Some of the leaders regularly travelled the affected areas, gave inciting speeches and created a new in them to arise, awake and march ahead. Some of them were eminent writers who supported their movement through the media. All of them were dedicated to the genuine cause of the peasants.

Conclusion

The peasant movement that occured in the United Provinces of Agra and Awadh for the first time expressed the discontent of a group that symbolized the common people. The patronage of politics helped the peasants to be orgainzed and united. But this movement was not a child of Indian political discontent or the national movement. In U.P. the peasant movements challenged the traditional rural order based upon age long exploitation of the priveleged upon the unpriveleged. No anti-imperialistic, the nationalistic consciousness originated it. It was definitely a movement from the below. It was in 1920 when the Home Rule League and the Indian National Congress began directing these movements and used therefore their own gains. The transformation of simple and spontaneous agrarian unrest into an organized peasant activity was not just sudden or an abrupt eruptin. The Congress tried to pacify the conflicting parties and a note of Zamindar Kisan amity also echoed in the midst of anti-landlordism of this move. The movement basically raised issues of injustice to the peasants at the hands of the zamindars and the government. The Talukadars were the landlords who gained very significant importance in the late 18th and 19th centuries due to their revenue functions. According to the British administrators they had undeniable rights in the soils and their lands were either ancestral or purchased or even acquired illegally through force. With the growth of the market for land in Awadh and Agra provinces, the Talukadars were transformed from powerful Rajas to powerful landlords. Some of the Talukadari estates were scattered over large areas and were not easy to manage. But the growing process of commercial agriculture created a pressure on the tillers.

The Revolt of 1857 joined the zamindars and peasants together and in the intoxicating foreover of the revolt the antigonism between the peasant and the zamindars were thrown out for the time being. The Viceroy Canning confiscated the proprietary rigthts in Awadh but the second settlement recognized the talukadar's proprietary rights. In 1866 the Awadh compromise was agreed upon and rights of occupancy was granted to those who had been earlier proprieters and who cultivated their ancestral fields. The compromise bill only exhibited that the Talukadar's approach was reasonable.

In 19th centuray, in the uneven spectrum of Talukadari estates, a special category emerged who had full proprietary rights as defined in the Awadh estates Act of 1869. They came to be known as the zmindars. Next were the under proprieters with whom sub settlements were made as Pukhtadars. Some fundamental social changes began to upset the precarious relationship of class, caste and power within the coloured framework. Lack of industries and other employment opportunities adversely affected the ratio between the man and the land.

Between 1870 and 1920 the population of Awadh grew in density per square mile to 504 and though it was not uniform in different areas, the districts of Faizabd, Pratapgarh, Sultanpur Barabanki and Rae Bareilly had great density of population. At these places the peasant movements had broken out. The main cause of the peasant movements therefore was the grim poverty of the lowest caste tenants and the agricultural labourers. The density of population added to its momentum because the people nourished a strong disinclination to move to a new spot. With no other a venue of employment the pressure on the land as well as the incresing revenue demand led to the fragmentation of the holdings. The desire to enhance rents resulted in the eviction of high caste cultivators. They were swept aside in the competition of commerce to make room for men of lower castes who agreed to pay a higher rent. Later this change caused strange outcomes.

The big zamindars and the traditional village Mahajan used to land money to the small land-holders and the peasants. The growth of indebtedness in Awadh among the large land-owners in some districts of U.P. due to their own mismanagement and heavy revenue demands. The estates were sold to repay the debts. Nothing was done to make improvements to help the cultivatiors in increasing the productivity. The landlords quickly forced them to evict the land and acted most irrationally.

It would be interesting to note the observation of Sleeman with regard ot the U.P. brahmins and other high caste people. They formerly did not drive their own ploughs but they begins driving themesleves. In fact the higher caste like Thakurs, Brahmans, Kayasthas and the Muhammadens considered it beneath their dignity to plough their own land. It ultimately led to a loss of rights and the usurpation of land by the bigger landlords or by the Mahajans. Many people of higher castes, having proprietary rights, adopted different professions.

The tyrannical landlords squeezed money from the tenants in the form of Nazrana or the tributes. There was no account properly or improperly kept and maintained for the Nazrana. The amount actually paid was not known to any of the officials. Nazarana was usually paid in the months of May, June and July just before eviction notices were to be served upon them. It was in the Awadh region of U.P. that the enormity of the rise in rents and Nazrana actually made the peasants more poor than before. It made them sociallly inferior and low. The transactions were cruelly made even when the agrarian system was at fault. The unrestrained exploitation of the zamindars became the most potent reason for the peasants revolts in the districts of U.P.

From 1860 to 1920, there was an all round rise in the prices of necessary commodities. It affected all the people of U.P., the rich and the poor alike. The agricultural labourers were adversely affected. There was no rise in the productivity. The peasants were not only oppressed on acount of heavy rent but they were prey to an entire situation. The rural society specially in the eastern U.P.

was a multiplex occupational society where there was no clear line of distinction between agricultural sector and other industries. The cultivators provided goods for everyday use and consumption at a rate which was for below the prevailing market rates.

The unrestricted power of the zamindars made them tough and stubborn. They thought wrongly that they could maintain their moral health leaving the entire society morally diseased. He became callous, imperious and cunning day by day. As a result the social tension in Awadh took a definte form of economic conflict between the different interests of the agrarian classes. The rapidly commercialized agriculture added fuel to the fire, and the rural regions of U.P. began to experience and unseen fire which quickly spread in western U.P.

In March 1861, the Talukadars had formed the British Indian Association of Awadh to help the British administratiors and they had acquired a new status as the supporters of the Raj. The British government recognized them as owners of the land. The peasantry of U.P. was obviouslly converted into tenantry. The Act of 1868 was a terrible blow to the peasantryof U.P. The Awadh Rent Act specially failed to proctect those tenants who most urgently needed the protection. When the increase in rents made the tenantry dependent on village Mahajans, a cruel social class was created and supported by practising lawyers, the police and the courts. The cruelities bitterly manifested itself in Murdafaroshi. Gorawan was another cruel tax imposed for the purchase of horse, for the purchase and maintenance of elephants. The talukadars extorted the Hathiana. There was another tax Biswa for the food of the elephant. Another cesses was Motrawan for purchasing a car. Nazar-e-Dama was charged from the tenants when the landlords visited the village. Durbars were held by them on festivals and the tenants were directed to pay Nazar or Bhent to their landlords. The tenants were checked form grazing their cattle in fields and forests without a tax.

The tenants were allowed to plant tree or grooves only when they obtained permission and paid the Nazrana. They were supposed to provide, one to three basket of 'Bhusa' to their landlords. They also gave free suger-canes and other products to the zamindar's family. The landlords also charged a nazrana if the tenants built a house or made any alteration or even occupy an empty house. The exploitation of Begar or free labour agitated the peasants. They were just slaves to zamindars. They were beaten with shoes and charged fine and finally ejected if the landlord was angry. When the government officials visited the Talukadari estate, the tenants were required to look for their comforts and supply every thing that he needed.

The tenant cultivators and other villagers were not allowed to live in the Taluk until they paid tributes to the Talukadars and their relatives. They used filthy languages against the tenants and treated them with contempt. The zilladars and the sipahis were the agents of the Talukadars and they behaved like the hungry hounds. If the tenants appealed in the court of law against the oppression and humiliation, they did not get any justice. Going to the courts was regarded as an act of enimity and the oppression doubled. When the first world war broke out, the miseries of the U.P. peasantry increased. They forced them of enlist in the army and to aid their imperial masters during the calamity. They forcibly recruited the jawans.

They collected subscription for the war fund. All this attributed to the rise of the peasants in U.P. as a militant group. Many of them had to sell their cattle to pay the amount of 'Sarkari Chanda'. The peasants were impoverished and frustrated totally.

There was one aspect that left a deep imprint on the so far explioted peasants. It was stated in the newspaper that for the first time the villagers as such became a significant unit of importance. The zamindars forced them for enlistment in the army and gave concessions to them for this favour. The agricultural disasters played havoc with the life of the agricultural labourers because they were left unemployed and they had nothing to depend upon.

When Jhunguri Singh and Sahdev Singh initiated a Kisan Sabha in Pratapgarh district, it channelized the peasants discontent and organized a mass movement to voice their demands and to affect their emancipation from talukadar's tyranny. An U.P. Kisan Sabha was also formed at Allahabad by the members of Home Rule Movement. It may be that the members expected to strangthen their own movement through the numerical point of view. The low castes were in the majority in the villages. The peasants families of Awadh were related to their castes in Agra province specially Allahabad and Jaunpur. They used to write letters to their relatives and informed them of the new organization of the peasants and also the contents of the letter of oath issued by the Kisan Sabha of Pratapgarh.

The leaders of the Home Rule Movement and the Indian National Congress activally played a double game, on the one hand they posed that they were offering urban leaderships to them, on the other they attempted for a compromise between peasants and the landlords. It appeared that the urban leadership attempted to exploit the peasnats discontent to further their own political party motives and ends. Yet the peasants came into the mainstream and began to be aware of the national issues.

Another Kisan Sabha was formed at Rasulpur where the tenants were subjected to ruthless oppression and they were annoyed with the local Talukadars. Leaders like Jawaharlal Nehru, Motilal Nehru, Abul Kalam Azad and Shaukat Ali visited the U.P. villages and advocated the cult of swaraj and non-cooperation among the peasants. But the crucial issues of concern to the peasantry were not included in their programme. The Awadh Kisan Sabha gradually spread its branches in Sultanpur, Faizabad and in other districts of U.P. It mobiulized its contacts with Rae Bareilly, Sultanpur, Faizabad and Lucknow and held huge rallies. The peasants were not satisfied with the peaceful demonstrations and petitions. They did not like the move of the leaders to reconcile with their enemies. They wanted to display their sterngth and frighten the zamindars, the money lenders and the British government.

In Nasirabad Tehsil of Salon in the district Rae Bareilly a fierce riot broke out. It was a mob swelled to ten thousand or more who looted and plundered the houses. They were armed with lathis axes, spears and bricks. The police opend fire in order to disburse them. Four peasants were killed, the anger of the crowd was against the Mahajans. It all took a fierce shape.

Another riot broke out at Munshi Ganj in the Rae Bareilly district. Many fakirs and pasis had joined them. Their leader was Fakir Rahmat Ali Shah. All the people in the violent crowd were wearing a coloured head dress. In Rae Bareilly district, violence broke out at Sehgaon and Pachmukhi village where the kurmi caste people attacked the police with lathis and spears. In this violence, there were certainly the elements of personal rivalry and enimity. Anothr armed revolt look place at Karhaiya bazar on the border of Rae Bareilly and Pratapgarh districts. It was also directed against the police which was regarded as the symbol of the government.

The armed revolts also broke out in Faizabad district. The tehsils of Akbarpur and Tanda were the most disturbed and the peasants looted and plundered the houses of the zamindars and the money lenders. The tenants who were quite dissatisfied were later joined by the agricultural labourers. All these voilent oubreaks in 1921 were the result of the tensions that prevailed in the rural areas against the landlords, money lenders and the government. The districts of Rae Bareilly, Sutanpur and Faizabad mainly experienced the violent riots. Every time the British police crushed them. It was mainly for the superior military forces at their command that they largely succeeded in suppressing them. The zamindars took up the advantage of their suppression by police. Numerous repression were filed in the court of law. The Awadh Kisan Sabha was more responsible for voilent riots than the U.P. Kisan Sabha.

The peasant movement proved to be an effective popular backing to the non-cooperation movemnet. The utility of this movement was well recognized by the Indian National Congress and the U.P. Congress Committee. Motilal Nehru as the President of the U.P. Kisan Sabha distributed a leaflet in the rural areas of U.P. containing the message of the need for dedication and sacrifice for the land. As it contained the signature of three young students they were immediately arrested and another faked pamphlets was distributed by the government asking the peasants to work silently for the additional Begaar. A few liberal associations were formed in U.P. for a view to reconcile the government and the peasants. Yet the Awadh Rent Bill was legislated on 4th of August 1921 raising the statutory period of tenancy from seven to ten years after which the rent was to be decided mutually or by the court. With the recommendations of the Committee, it was hotly debated. The presented resented the Bill and the role of Liberals therein. The failure of the non-cooperation movement too doomed the peasants movemnet and it became of a reduced nature.

The Eka Movement which started in the district of Hardoi in the end of 1921 mainly protested against the non receipt payments. It had spread in Baharaich, Lucknow, Sitapur and Barabanki. The movement was made strong by the sanctity of an elaborate ritual by digging a hole representing the river Ganga and all the rebellious peasants took an oath over it amidst recital of mantras by the village pandit who was paid by them. The organisation multiplied splendidly. Though there was no co-ordination leadership of this movemnt. The government called them as dacoits. It was primarily a tenant's movement. The politics of the non-cooperation did not influence them much. It had some effect of khilafat ideas but it was also later shunned. Some Khilaftist zamindars had extended in advertently their support to Eka Movement of the peasants. However it was mainly low caste tenants movement under the guidance of Madari and Sohrab. It was crushed within four month and did not revive again.

In northern India specially in U.P. the British revenue law was very well defined and clear. It lied not in the land itself but in the right to levy revenue from it. The Malguzari right could readily become separated off as a form of ground rental property leaving the physical control of the land in the hands of other. The rural society refused to be neatly segregated into the mutually exclusive roles of the landlord, tenant, labourer and doubled and trebled these roles endlessly, the vast majority of the cultivators in United provinces of Agra and Awadh were classified legally as tenants. They devised that all the unprotected tenants should be accorded occupaney status. The indebtedness had thrown the cultivation into most serious dependence on the non-agriculturalist and tormented potentia civil discord in agriculturally insecure tracts or in densely settled pockets of the poorer tenants.

The peasants risings in U.P. was a complex affair in the sense that these violent outbursts mirrored their resentment at social displacement caused by the loss of their control over the land to the richer and newer faces and sometimes to the urban money lending castes. It was indirectly dircted against the government.

In the begining the toughest peasants resitance came from the groups in the villages that warded of the threats of eviction. The British administrators collaborated with the smaller Rajas and tried to control the wealth of the peasants with polite behaviour.

The shift in the land owning castes was indeed remarkable. At places where caste homogeneity was lacking, the landlords became more sever and grasping than over before. Some of these estates were notoriously known for their oppressive management. Nothing more could be expented of the rural setting in the colonial India except the exploitation of the poor peasants at its height.

It was after 1856 that the alien government started backing the Talukadars of Awadh and recognized them as the legal proprietors of the land. They paid to the government approximately half the value of the gross rental of an estate each year as land revenue. Occasional and illegal lootings of the Talukadars on their peasantry gave way to a legal levy of land revenue demnad by the government. It resulted in a top heavy landlordism that created further pressure on the peasantry. One half of the gross rental in the rural regions were taken over by the State. Lack of agricultural technology was the basis for the low produce and the sluggish agrarian society in which the peasants lived unable to pay his land revenue the landowner demanded more rent from the tenants. He also reduced the tenant's share in the gross produce. It perpetuated the slugghishness and left much less with tillers of the soil for their subsistence. The colonial agrarian economy resulted in the rise of prices of the chief superior and also inferior food grains. All this added agony and pain in the peasant's life.

In Awadh the peasants joined together on the basis of caste. The existence of castes in rural societies helped the peasant movement of Awadh and they united together in a strong bond of brotherhood and fellow feeling. It would not be wrong to conclude that, it was a movement of the poor classes and its causes were mainly economic. Besides it was a movement of the deprived and low castes like 'Pasi', 'Kurmi', 'Faquirs' and Sanyasis. They were wrongly specified as criminals by the government officials. The caste panchayats ordered for the social boycott to such peasants as did not join the movement, though they were of the same caste. Their castes feared the panchayat's decision but did not bother for the law courts. Many genuine peasant leaders were crushed by the British police in the name of anti-social elements.

It is sigificant to note that ultimately the peasants were diverted to the movement organized either by the Indian National Congress or the Communist Party. In fact the peasants movements had spontaneous origin and the violent out bursts were never predicted or planned earlier. It had different causes at different places and at different time. The movement from below was given much boost by its cohesion with the congress politics. The Congress leaders became quite interested in the progress of the peasant movements and they helped them to stand on their own feet. By 1921 the U.P Kisan Sabha was divided into two camps. The Awadh Kisan Sabha began to take keen interest in the Non-cooperation Movement and other programmes of the Indian National Congress and the United Provinces Congress Committee. But the liberals percived the interest of the peasants. The U.P.C.C. also declared that it would take up the work of labour and peasant and peasant classes and organize these to massive majority. But later they could not define their own concepts regarding these issues and they were fearful of the Russian ideology that entered into these organizations. Often in the name of non violence, the leaders of the Congress tried to reconcile the two poles of the Talukadars and the tenants. Not only that they failed but they were exposed badly.

There was often a dichotomy troubling the peasants thesmelves and making them helpless and mute. Their demands that were based upon the support of the landless tenants and agricultural labourer were not supported either by the Awadh Kisan Sabha or the U.P. Kisan Sabha. The Eka Movement was one which supported their cause but neither the liberals not the Congress came to strengthen it. A few Congress leaders and the Khilafatist only in the beginning were seen taking interest in its activities. When the polarization became acture in Eka too, that is the kisans on one side and the zaminars on the other, the Congress attempted a reconciliation between them. They did not like to lose either of them. But these efforts for feited the objectives of the peasants movement.

Though the life of the peasants movements in U.P. was not very long, it cannot be over looked and it indeed deserves all praise and admiration. Their natural responsed to the British colonial exploitation appears unique and great. The lack of perfect leadership and a well chalked out programme, in fact, defeated the massive movements so laboriously organized by the peasants on their own. However it troubled the scheming and greedy zamindars who were the real instruments of the British imperialism. The British government was too afraid of them lest they might get help from the Bolsheviks of U.S.S.R. The mushroom growth of the Kisan Sabhas in most of the districts of U.P. totally upset the Britishers and they started entangling the leaders of the peasant movement in false case of dacoity and loot.

To sum up the peasants movements of U.P. were the conscious and deliberate attempt at building up a peasant organization for drawings up the attention of the alien rulers to the various form of agrarian agression and exploitation that existed for long. They started the grass root peasant activity with the expansion of the Kisan Sabhas under local leadership in various villages. A galaxy of peasant leaders emerged who were self-trained in the school of depravation and poverty. They were not like the white collared leadership of the Congress and they did not have strong support of the urban elites. They just sprang up amidst problems of local nature yet they bravely faced the cruelties of the alien governments. They had a grip on the masses and they lad them quite ably.

The attainments of the peasants movement cannot be denied. In this reports and despatches, the British authorities often insisted on granting concessions to them. But the cruel zamindars, who were the supporters of the British imperialistic motives were not ready to part with there age long privileges and they exploited the poor peasants and squeezed them to the full. In such a setting, the courgae and bravery of the lower strata of tenants must be widely acknowledged. After all, the humans as they were, they broke their age long silence and their fiery eruptions shot up. Not only the palatial mansions of the cruel zamidars were burnt but also the iron administration of the British government began to shake with fear.

A vast majority of the U.P. peasants learnt to participate in the national movement and attended the annual sessions of the Indian National Cogress. They ultimately became the stounch supporters of 'Swaraj' for the country. They had become the masses behind Gandhiji. They later on, mingled into the national main stream of the struggle for Indian independence and sacrificed their lives for the national cause.

An impartial evaluation of the peasants' movement in U.P. convinces about the selflessness of the peasant leaders and about the genuine grievances that they raised before the alien government. It also outlines the selfish motive of the Congress leaders to use the peasants masses for their own party. The Indian freedom struggle actually became a mass movement when the peasants and labourers joined it. The Congress was not only strengthened numerically but it could reach the villages and remote areas and could convince them of the efficacy of truth and non-violence. The innocent but hard working peasants who did not know any ideology of communism were labeled to be the followers of red flag.

But neither did they attempt to understand the ideology nor did they believe in a revolution of communist type. Actually they were not enough educated to understand those high principles. All that they came forward to do was to struggle against the socio-economic attrocites of those who exploited them since the very beginning. Their violence was in reply to the violence of the exploiters. The leaders of the movement were the people who were theistic, dedicated to Indian culture and religion. They suffered a lot but they stood firm against injustice, cruelties and exploitation. They wrote the history of the lower classes in golden words. They exhibited to the world that it is not necessary to always crush down the poor and lower castes and classes. They showed their strength to their opponents—the zamindars and the government and that to such an extent that proved indeed amazing and decisive.

Bibliography

Primary Sources

AICC (All India Congress Committee) File No. 4, The U.P. Provincial Congress Committee and the Economic Distress in the Rural areas in the Provinces.

Agrarian Distress in the United Provinces U.P. Congress Committee, Allahabad 1931.

Census Report of 1921 for the United Provinces, Part II.

Census of India, 1921 United Provinces of Agra and Oudh, Vol. XVI, Part 1, Report (Allahabad)1923.

Home (Political) Department, Government of India, File No. 75 (1920), 18(1922) 1-28 (January, 1928) 17-29 (February-June 1929), 18/5/31 May 1931, 18/5/32 (Pol) March 1932, 18/8/1939, 18/6/1944.

Indigo Cultivation in Bengal, Parliamentary Papers (1861), Vol. XLI.

The Indian Quarterly Register, Calcutta, Vol III, July-December, 1927.

Imperial Gazetter of India, Vol. XIX.

International Press Correspondance (Berlin) Vol. 2 /No. 51 20/6/1922 M.N. Roy.

Oudh Revenue Administration Report (ORAR) 1880-81.

Papers Relating to Land Tenures and Revenue Settlement in Awadh.

Pratapgarh Settlement Report, 1896.

Police Abstract of Intelligence 04/03/1922, CID recodrs Lucknow.

Report of the Special Session of the Indian National Congress held in Delhi.1918.

Rae Bareilly Settlement Report 1872.

Reoprt on the working of the system of Governmnet of United Provinces of Agra and Oudh, 1921-28, Allahabad.

Report of the Delhi Provincial Political Confrence (13-15 October) President Pt. Nehru and held at Meerut.

Telegram No. 21 F, Dated Lucknow 7th January 1921, from the Chief Secretary to Govt. of the United Provines, Home (Pol). Department File No 17.

Terrorism is Sitapur District in All India Congress Committee, File No. 5/1922.

United Provinces, Legislative Council Proceedings 1921, Vol.5.

II - Secondary Sources (Books, News Papers and Articles) 1 Books

A. R. Desai (ed.) "*Rural Sociology in India*", Bombay, Popular Prakashan, 1969.

A. R. Desai (ed.), "*Peasant Struggles in Indi*a", Bombay, OUP, 1979.

A. Bhaduri, "Agricultural Backwardness - Under Semi-Feudalism", *The Economic Jouranal*, 1973.

Asia Siddiqui, "*Agrarian Change in a Northern Indian State, 1819-33*, Oxford, 1973.

B. C. Ghosal, "*Some Notes on Raj Nanpara or the Tragic Story of the Premier Mohammedan Estate in Oudh,* Lucknow, 1918.

B. H. Baden Powell, "The Indian Village Community" (London,1869). 7; B. H. Baden Powell, "*Land Systems of British India*, Vol.II, Oxford Clarendon Press 1972".

B. R. Misra, "*Land Revenue Policy in United Provinces Under British Rule*."

C. A. Baylx, "*The Local Roots of Indian Politics, 1880-1920*, Allahabad, Oxford, 1975.

D. A. Low (ed.), "*Congress and the Raj 1917-47*, London, Arnold Heineman,1977.

D. N. Dhangre, "*Agrarian Movements and Gandhian Politics*, Agra, 1975.

D. N. Dhangre," Congress and Agrarian Agitation in Oudh,1920-22 and 1930-32, *Journal of South Asian Studies*, 1975.

D. N. Dhangre, "*Peasant Movements in India, 1920-50*, Delhi, OUP, 1983.

D. Rothermind, "*Government, Landlords and Peasant in India", Agrarian Relations Under British Rule, 1865-1935.*

Daulat Singh and V. K. Singh, "*Changing Agrarian Relations in India*, Hyderabad, NICD, 1975.

E. J. Hobssbawmn and others (ed.), *Peasant in History: Essays in Honour of Danial Tharner*, Calcutta, OUP, 1980.

E. T Atkinson, *Statistical Descriptive and Historical Account of N. W. Provinces.*

Eric Stokes, *The English Utilitarians and India, 1801-33.*

Eric Stokes, The Strucutre of Land holding in Uttar Pradesh, 1860-1948, *IESHR*, Vol. 12, No.2, June 1975.

Eric Stokes, The Peasant Armed, The Indian Revolt of 1857, Oxford, 1986.

Gyanendra Pandey, *The Ascendancy of Congress in Uttar Pradesh, 1926-34, A Study in Imperfect Mobilization*, Delhi OUP, 1978.

Gyanendra Pandey, *Peasant Revolt and Indian Nationalism, The Peasant Movement in Oudh*, 1919-22.

G. S. Bhalla, Peasant Movement and Agrarian Change in India, SS, Vol.ll No. 8, August, 1982.

Govind S. Kalkar, *Kisan Unrest and the Congress in Uttar Pradesh,* 1920-22.

Hamza Alavi, "Peasant and Revolution" The Socialist Register 1965. 26. Harold A., Gould , "Politics of Agrarian - Unrest in U.P. who Co-opted whom? *EPW,* Vol. 19 N. 19, December 8,1984.

Harcourt Butler, *Oudh Policy: The Policy of Sympathy*, Allahabad 1906.

Harcourt Butler, *Oudh Policy Considered Historically with reference to the present, Political Situation*, Allahabad, 1896.

H. C. Irwin, "*The Garden of India" or Chapters on Oudh History and Affairs,* London, 1880.

Imtiaz Hussain, "*British Land Revenue Policy in Northern India*", 1801-03, Calcutta, 1967.

Irfan Habib, "*The Peasant in Indian Histroy*", Vol. II No. 3, March, 1983.

Indian National Congress, U.P. Provincial Congress Committee Agrarian Distress in the Untied Provences (being the Report of Committee Appointed in 1931), Gurgaon, Prabha Publication.

INC, U.P.P.C.C. : Congress Agrarian Enquiry Committee Report, 1936 (United Provinces) Haryana, Prabha Publications.

J. Nehru, *An Autobiography*, London, 1936.

Jawaharlal Nehru, "*Discovery of India*", Bombay,, 1961.

Joan P. Mencher (ed), *Social Anthropology of Peasantry,* Bombay, Somaya Publications, 1983.

Kathaleen Guff, "Indian Peasant Uprisings", *Economic and Political Weekly*, Bombay, Special Number, 1974.

Katheleen Guf, Indian Village Communities and Peasant Movenents in India.

K. Gopalan Kutti, "The Integration of Anti-Landlord Movement with the Movement against imperialism.

Kapil Kumar, Peasant Participation of Gandhi and his Programme: Oudh 1920-22, Vol.II, No.2, February, 1983.

Kapil Kumar, *Peasaant in Revolt: Tenants Landlords, Congress and the Raj in Oudh, 1886-1922*, New Delhi, Manohar Prakashan, 1984.

M. A. Rasul, "*A History of All Indian Kisan Sabha*, Calcutta, National Book Agency, 1974"

M. B. Pandy, *Oudh Ke Kisanon Ki Durdasha*, Allahabad, 1921.

Majid Hayat Siddiqui, *Agrarian Unrest in North India, The United Provinces, 1918-22*, New Delhi, OUP, 1978.

M. H. S., The Peasant Movement in Pratapgarh, 1920, *IESHR* Vol.9 No.3, September 1972.

M. P. Saxsena. "Rent Law in Oudh, Hardoi, 1938.

N.G. Ranga, *Revolutionary Peasants*, New Delhi, Amrit Book Co., 1949.

Ranjit Guha, "*Elementary Aspects of Peasants Insurgency in Colonial India*, Delhi, OUP, 1983."

Ranjit Guha (ed), *Subaltern Studies-III*: Writings on South Asian History and Society, New Delhi, OUP, 1982-94.

R.C.Majumdar, *The Sepoy Mutiny and the Revolt of 1857*, 2nd edn. Calcutta (1963).

R. E. Frykenberg (ed), *Land Control and Social Structure in Indian History*, Wisconsin, 1969.

R. Sarvadhi Kari, *The Talukdari Settlement in Oudh*, Calcutta 1882.

R. P. Dutt, *India Today* (London) 1940.

Ram Subas, Dynamics of Agrarian Relations in Sultanpur, Eastern U. P., Vol. 12, No. 7 July 1984.

S. B. Chaudhary, *Civil Distrubances During the Britishg Rule in India*, Calucutta, 1958.

Sukhbeer Choudhari, "Peasant and Workers Movemet in India, 1905-1929.

S. B. Chaudhary, "*Civil Rebellion in the Mutinies*, Calcutta, 1857.

Smita Jassal, "Agrarian Contrdictions and Resistance in Faizabad, District of Oudh (India) 1858-1970, *J.P.S.* Vol.7 No. 3, April 1980.

S.K. Mittal and Kapil Kumar, Anti-Feudal and Anti Colonial Struggle of the Oudh peasantry in Early 1920, Vol.8, No. 12 July 1980.

S.K.Mittal and Kapil Kumar, Baba Ram Chandra and Peasant Upsurge in Oudh 1920-21, Vol.6, No. 11 June, 1978.

Sulekh Chandra Gupta, "Agrarian Relations and Early British Rule in India: A case study of Ceded and Conquered Provinces (Uttar Pradesh) 1801-1833. Bombay, APH, 1963.

S. N. Sen, Eighteen Fifty Seven, Calcutta, 1957.

S. B. Chaudhary, "Theories of Indian Mutiny, Calcutta, 1965.

S. A. A. R. Rizvi (ed), "Freedom Stuggle in Uttar Pradesh.

S. Gopal (ed), *Selected Work of Jawahar Lal Nehru*, Vol. I, New Delhi, 1972.

S.N.A. Jafri, "History and Status of Landlords and Tenants in the United Provinces, Allahabad, 1931.

Siddique Ahmed, Tarikh Anjuman Hind Oudh, Vol. III, Lucknow, 1937.

T. R. Metcalf, "The Aftermath of Revolt, India, 1857-70.

U.P. Zamindari, Abolition Committee Report, Allahabad 1948.

U.P. Banking Enquiry Committee Reports, 1929-30, Calcutta, 1930.

V. D. Savarkar, The Indian War of Independence of 1857, London, 1909.

W.F. Crowley, "Kisan Sabhas and Agrarian Revolts in the U.P.", Modern Asian Studies, 1971.

W. Crooke, Natives of Northern India, London, 1907.

W.H. Moreland, "Revenue Administration of the United Provinces", Allahabad 1931.

W.C. Bennett, "Gazetteer of the Province of Oudh, Lucknow, 1877.

P.C. Joshi, Rebellion of 1857, A Symposiam, New Delhi, 1957.

P.D. Reeves (ed)," Sleeman in Oudh, An Abridgement of W. H. Sleemans" A Journey through the Kingdom of Oudh 1849-50, Cambridge, 1971.

P.J. Musgrave, "An Unseen Hand ? Rural Credit and Rural Society in the United Provinces, 1860-1920.

P.J. Musgrave, "Landlords and Lords of the Land" Estate Management and Social Control in U.P. 1860- 1920. (Modern Asian Studies).

II-- News Papers

Abhudya, (Weekly, Allhabad).

Hindu Patriot.

Independent (Allhabad).

Indian Mirror (Daily).

Leader (Allhabad).

Pioneer.

Times of India.

Index